THE GOLDSMITH OF FLORENCE

A Cabasset. Italian, Late XVI Century.

THE GOLDSMITH ✠ OF FLORENCE ✠

A BOOK OF GREAT CRAFTSMEN

By
KATHARINE GIBSON
Decorations By
KALMAN KUBINYI

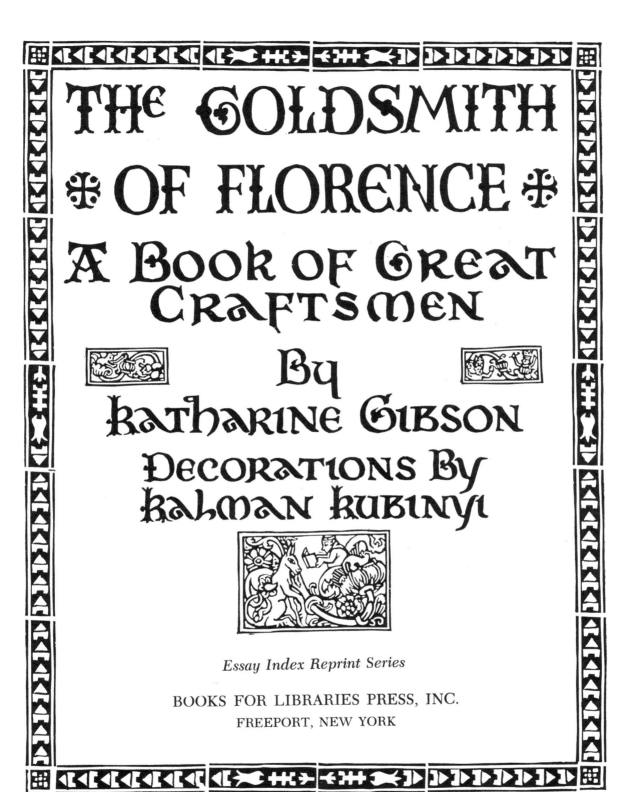

Essay Index Reprint Series

BOOKS FOR LIBRARIES PRESS, INC.
FREEPORT, NEW YORK

·First published 1929
Reprinted 1967

LIBRARY OF CONGRESS CATALOG CARD NUMBER:
67-30215

PRINTED IN THE UNITED STATES OF AMERICA

To

SARAH BERRY GILBERT

MY GRANDMOTHER, WHO IN HER NINETY-
EIGHTH YEAR IS THE YOUNGEST AND MOST
ENTHUSIASTIC READER I SHALL EVER HAVE

ACKNOWLEDGMENTS

I wish to express my sincere appreciation to Charles Scribner's Sons for permission to quote from the Blashfield-Hopkins edition of Vasari's "Lives of the Painters"; to Brentano's for permission to quote from "The Life of Benvenuto Cellini Written by Himself," edited and translated by John Addington Symonds; to The Page Company, Boston, for permission to quote from "Arts and Crafts in the Middle Ages," by Julia de Wolf Addison; to Henry Frowde, Oxford University Press, London, for permission to adapt material from "Wood Carving in English Churches, I. Misericords," by Francis Bond.

I am under obligations to Mr. I. Kirchmayer and Mr. Frank L. Koralewsky for their kind help in the chapters, "A Wood-Carver of To-day" and "Master Smith," and for the gift of photographs used in these two chapters; to Mr. H. C. Perleberg, publisher, for the gift of a plate from "Russian Peasant Art," by Count A. A. Bobrinsky; to W. A. Call, The County Studio, Monmouth, England, for assistance in procuring illustrative material on English misericords; to Mr. Hollis French, The Cluny Museum, The Kaiser Friedrich Museum, The Victoria and Albert Museum, The Metropolitan Museum of Art, the Museum of Fine Arts, Boston, and The Cleveland Museum of Art for permission to reproduce photographs.

I desire especially to thank Mr. Stephen V. Grancsay, Associate Curator of Armor, In Charge, The Metropolitan Museum, for his help on the chapter, "The Armorer"; Mrs. Anna Wyers Hill, for her graciousness in sharing her knowledge as a practical craftsman; Mr. Rossiter Howard, Assistant Director in The Cleveland Museum of Art, for his willingness to review the entire book; and all those members of the Museum Staff who have interested themselves in this attempt. I wish, also, to express my gratitude to Miss Sybil Cox for her very competent help in making suggestions and corrections in the manuscript.

CONTENTS

PART I

PART II

PART III

ILLUSTRATIONS

ILLUSTRATIONS

ILLUSTRATIONS

In the Time of the Knights
A Foreword

Every one knows how the knights of long ago glittered in their armor, what pride they took in their swords, how the ladies of the courts of the Middle Ages spent long hours over their beautifully written and painted books while their lords were away at the wars. Every one knows that kings sat proudly on carven thrones, watching, as they sat, the gayly woven figures upon tapestried walls.

But of the men who labored that such things should be, of the weaver, the illuminator of books, the wood-carver, and the armorer much less is known. The first four chapters of this book try to tell a little of these nameless men and of how they worked.

Weavers of Stories Tapestries

WEAVERS OF STORIES

Long ago, the folk depended upon pictures for much of their learning. In the thirteen, fourteen, and fifteen hundreds, it was not every man who could read. Only those few who had gone to the monasteries and learned from the good monks knew their letters. The commoner, and often the rich burgher, and sometimes even the knight and the nobleman were fortunate if they could write their names. To have pictures was not so simple either, as there were, of course, no printing presses and pictures were rarely reproduced. They were found in Italy in the churches, painted on plaster, wood, and, later on, canvas; and in France and England they were often made of glass. The great windows in the churches were called "the Bibles of the poor." For from these glowing, jewel-like surfaces the who could not read studied the old Bible tales.

There was another important way in which stories were told. They were told in wool by the weavers of tapestry. The castle walls and the walls of the churches in France, in England, in Holland and Flanders were of stone, cold and cheerless in winter. In order to give them color, great hangings were made. Suspended on heavy iron hooks driven into the stones, they brought warmth and beauty into many a hall which would have been grim indeed without them. It is hard to trace exactly how these tapestries came to be woven in the north countries. It seems likely, however, that the industry came, as did so much else, from the church or the monasteries. The good monks, and in some cases the nuns, set up up their looms and worked with their simple piles of wool, their bobbins, and their combs before the busy folk in the town had any notion of such undertakings.

It was not many years, however, until in the cities of Flanders and northern France there were thriving companies of men who made their living by weaving tapestries. Arras, a Flemish town during the days of its greatness, was one of the foremost centers for this industry. Indeed, this city gave its name to its products; and frequently a weaving is known as an *arras* instead of a *tapestry*.

The painters of the world's great pictures are well known, and the facts of their lives have been, in most instances, carefully recorded. But with weavers it is all very

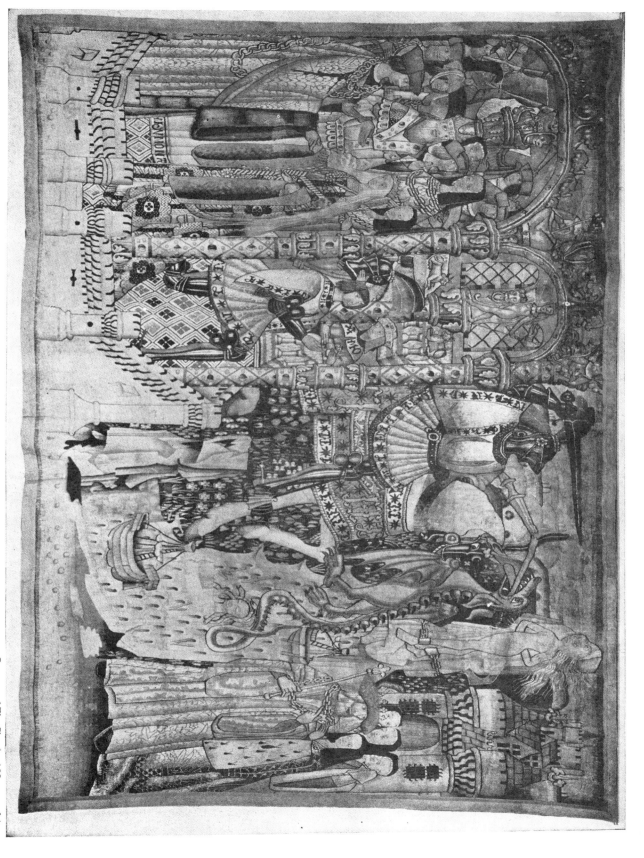

The Perseus and Andromeda Tapestry. Franco-Flemish, 1480.

Courtesy of The Cleveland Museum of Art.

different. In old lists, in certain transactions between merchants, are found here and there the names of master weavers. But as to how they lived, what were their adventures, their likes and dislikes, their fortunes good or bad, little is remembered. The beholder, looking at the great tapestries that have survived the years, finds only the skill, the patience, the training, the knowledge of the weaver. In almost every instance the man himself has disappeared. He did his work, literally wove out his life with the bobbin he held in his hand, and is gone. Yet in a sense he lives more truly than many a one whose name has come down in history charged with deeds both black and glowing. The weaver has left only the record of his best; in this perhaps he is the more fortunate and the more to be honored.

If such a weaver is to be known, he must be known chiefly with the imagination. Give him a name for old times' sake. Pierre will do as well as any other. This Pierre lived perhaps just after the good days of Arras had gone by, just after it was conquered by the French king, Louis XI. And so Pierre left his native city. He lived at a time when Brussels was becoming the center for tapestries. Pierre, however, did not choose to settle in Brussels. His memories of the happy years in Arras were too strong. He became, as did so many of his fellows, a wandering or itinerant weaver. With his bobbins, his comb, and his simple roll of clothing on his back, he went now to Lille, now to Paris, and perhaps even into Italy.

A thin little man, maybe, bent from so many hours over the loom, he was dressed in doublet and hosen with a warm cloak to cover him from rain and wind. He had keen eyes that saw a whole story in an inch of good weaving. He had fine, long-fingered hands, kept smooth and soft so that his wools would neither snarl nor catch. His head was full of old romances, of parables from the Bible, of Greek myths. He was no machine. He put thought and affection into every tale that he made, did this weaver of stories.

Sitting before some great loom in a strange town far from his native Arras, working for some strange patron, the old workman bent to his task. He did not count hours or days. Weeks passed into months. Gradually, very gradually, however, the web grew under his hand. The subject of his work? No one knows. But in imagination it may be said quite correctly that the tapestry here pictured, "Perseus and Andromeda," was woven by the imaginary Pierre. As he sat at his loom, Pierre thought of the story, how Perseus was the son of the Greek god Zeus and Danaë.

Acrisius, father of Danaë, being warned that his daughter's son would be the cause of his death, had Danaë and her new-born babe put into the sea in an open chest. The chest

The Lady and the Unicorn, Sight. French, about 1495.

floated toward Seriphus, where it was found by a fisherman, who took the child and his mother to Polydectes, king of the country. Polydectes in time desired Danaë for his wife. She sternly rejected his suit. The king, thinking that he might be more successful if Perseus, now grown to manhood, were out of the way, decided to dispatch the young hero on a most perilous adventure. He sent Danaë's son to slay the Gorgon, Medusa.

The Gorgon had been a most lovely maiden, so beautiful, in fact, that she had claimed even greater charms than those of the goddess, Hera. In punishment for this boldness, Hera had Medusa's golden hair changed to hundreds of hissing snakes. So terrible was she that if any living creature gazed but once upon Medusa, it was immediately turned to stone.

When the gods on Mount Olympus heard of the hazardous adventure of Perseus, they came to his aid. Hermes brought his winged sandals; Dis, his helmet of invisibility; Athena, her gleaming shield. "O Perseus," said the gray-eyed one, "when you approach the Gorgon, gaze not upon her fearfulness; turn your head away, and looking in the shield at her reflection pictured there, raise then your sword and strike."

Perseus listened carefully to the directions given him by the immortal three; then, donning his helmet, girding on his sword, strapping his sandals, and grasping his shield firmly, he rose into the air. Birds fled terrified at the sound of his winged feet; looking, they could see nothing, could only feel a presence passing them with deadly speed. When he reached the friendless spot where the Gorgons dwelt, he remembered well the commands of the gods. Lifting high his sword, he slew the fearful image which he saw writhing in the mirror made by his well-polished shield.

On his return journey, Perseus with the head of Medusa safely hidden in a great bag was flying along the coast of the country of the Æthiopians. There he spied a beautiful maiden chained to a rock. He would have thought her a marble statue save for her falling tears and her fair hair blowing across her like a garment of fine-spun gold. Her mother, Cassiopeia, proud of her beauty, had dared to compare herself to the sea nymphs. This so roused their wrath that they sent a great monster to ravage all the land. To appease the monster, Cepheus, king of Æthiopia, was told by an oracle to offer up his only daughter Andromeda. The maiden, trembling, related her tragic fate to Perseus; and even as she spoke, the waves parted and the scaly body of the monster appeared. The maiden gave a shriek. Like a falling star Perseus again dropped upon his foe and slew it with his mighty sword. In gratitude for this daring act, Cepheus gave his daughter in marriage to Perseus and celebrated the event with a magnificent wedding-feast.

In time Perseus and Andromeda came again to Seriphus. There Perseus revenged the king's treatment of his mother by showing him the fatal Gorgon and changing him to stone. He then returned to the gods their great and magic gifts, fixing the head of Medusa on Athena's shield where it may be seen today. Danaë now longed to visit her own country. So with Perseus and Andromeda she journeyed on to Argos. Perseus found that his grandfather had been driven from his throne by a usurper. He slew the unlawful king and restored the aged Acrisius to the throne. But the old prophecy came true. Perseus was playing at quoits one morning with his friends. Acrisius, standing near by, was accidentally struck by the discus and killed. Perseus then became king, though he grieved at the slaying of his grandfather. He ruled the land well; and at their death he and Andromeda joined the immortals.

[6]

The Lady and the Unicorn, Hearing. French, about 1495.

On the right-hand side of the tapestry, which is quite large—nearly ten by fifteen feet—the parents of Andromeda stand sadly awaiting the fearful end of their daughter. The court are gathered, weeping her fate. In the distance are the French towers, which, curiously, formed part of Andromeda's Æthiopian home. Andromeda with her floating hair is chained to the rock. The sea flows at her feet. Upon it are medieval ships, suggesting the journey of Perseus; and the Gorgon with her snaky locks is quaintly pictured. The central figure, the knight in full armor and surcoat, is, of course, Perseus. His sword is uplifted. With his lance he has pierced the throat of the monster, who is indeed a strange-looking beast. In the archway to the left of the central group, Perseus kneels, probably making an offering and a prayer that he may succeed in his great venture. His squire stands behind him. Under the final arch is the marriage scene. The bishop in his brocaded robes is performing the ceremony, while the parents and the court stand in the background rejoicing that their princess and their country have been saved.

In the Perseus tapestry the hero appears not as a Greek warrior, but as a knight in armor. Andromeda wears not the chiton of the women of Argos, but the court costume of about 1480. It was a habit of the old French and Flemish weavers like Pierre—along with the other artists of their time—to clothe the people in their stories not in the costume they would naturally have worn, but in the cloaks and robes the artists saw about them every day. It is as though some one should make a picture of George Washington at Valley Forge and present him wearing the uniform of General Pershing. These tapestries, then, are a strange mixture of Greek myth and of the life of the time in which they were woven.

Nowhere else in the world can so much be learned about the life of the Middle Ages as in these wall hangings. There are the costumes, the customs, the games, the battles, the legends, the romances, which were a part of daily life and thought. In the Perseus story, you have a double interest, the interest of the old classic tale and the interest in the lives of the knights and ladies pictured so faithfully.

The method by which Pierre did his weaving is worth knowing about. Long ago, long before the days of the Arras weavers, the first looms were made of two uprights with a straight piece across the top to which many threads were attached. These threads were weighted at the bottom with stones. The weaver stood and wove his cloth from top to bottom or toward him.

Then one day some unknown genius had an idea. The stick at the top was replaced by a roller, and a second roller was added at the bottom. Now the weaver could attach his threads at both ends, they could be held firmly in place, and the

The Lady and the Unicorn, Smell. French. about 1495.

finished cloth could be rolled on the lower roller. The weaver now wove from *bottom* to *top*, or away from him. This loom is known as the high-warp loom.

The high-warp loom was by no means the last step in inventiveness. One day a clever man turned his loom over like a table. He attached treadles to it so that part of his work could be done with his feet. This made the task go much more swiftly, and it did not greatly reduce the quality of the weaving if the tapestry were made by a skilled workman. This loom was known as a low-warp loom. As with the later type of high-warp loom the weaver weaves away from him upon the low-warp.

Whether high- or low-warp loom is being discussed, the threads fastened on the roller are called *warp* threads. They were usually of hemp. The weaver held in his hand a bobbin. This was wound with a long wool thread; for each color he had to have a separate bobbin. He fastened one end of his woolen or *weft* thread to a warp thread and worked horizontally across the loom. With the little pointed nose of the

High-Warp Loom.

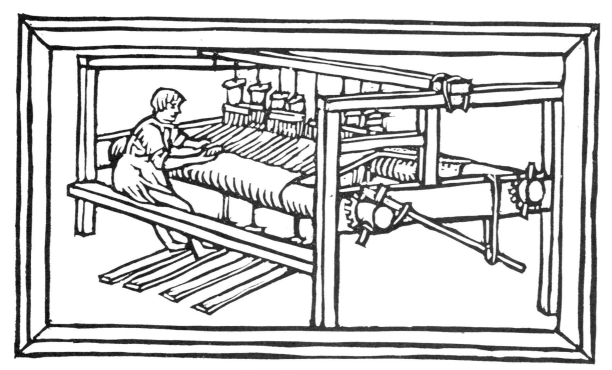

Low-Warp Loom.

bobbin he felt his way, going over and under, and covering the hemp or warp threads with the wool or weft threads.

The worker wove a small patch at a time, now a bit of red, now a bit of blue, gradually building up his pattern. When he had finished a few rows, he took his little weaver's comb and pressed them compactly together. One of his most difficult tasks was the blending of his colors. This he did by what is known as *hatching*. Any one looking at an old tapestry carefully is apt to find many places where one color is worked into another just as a drawing is shaded; there are fine lines of white on blue, of red on green, of green on yellow. If the hatching is done skillfully, the tapestry is rich and glowing. If not, it looks spotty, much like the crazy quilts that our grandmothers used to make.

The old French and Flemish weavers used comparatively few colors, fifteen or twenty at the most, while the modern weaver in the great looms at Paris today has some 14,400 shades at his command. Strange to say the older workers were the more fortunate. A wall hanging with a few, simple, beautifully dyed wools was, after all, the most restful and the most satisfactory. The dyes were all vegetable, many of them made from plants growing in the weavers' own countryside. They were often made in comparatively small quantities; and occasionally while a tapestry was being woven, a new vat of red, blue, or green had to be mixed and did not match exactly. In this way the old things have a pleasant variation which is lacking in our machine-made fabrics.

Silver and even gold threads were used in weaving the tapestry, but the most important material was wool. Then, as now, the best wool came from England; and of the English wool the finest, from Kent. The city of Antwerp in Flanders was the great center of import and export. Here came the great bales of fleece from English pastures; here came the finished rolls of tapestry from the towns of France and Flanders. Here they were put in ships and sent all over the world as presents to emperors and kings of Europe, to sultans and caliphs of the Far East.

Now the tapestries were not woven according to the weaver's fancy; this would have been quite impossible. Patterns were made, often by great artists. These were called *cartoons*. In the case of the high-warp loom they were hung up behind the weaver; with the low-warp loom they were placed underneath the warp threads, and the workman looked through the threads at his model. As an additional help, the general outline of the pattern or cartoon was traced on the warp threads of the tapestry. With both high- and low-warp looms the weaver wove on the wrong side. With the high-warp loom, if he wanted to see the right side, he had only to get up and walk to the front of the loom; with the low-warp loom, however, he had to wait until the work was completed before he could see the right side. In either case the weaver had to depend upon skill and experience as his chief guide.

There is a group of tapestries in The Cluny Museum in Paris known as "The Lady and the Unicorn" series because they all deal with one general theme or subject. They were woven in France about the year 1495. Again it is quite safe to think of the worker as an imaginary one, this time perhaps Marc. No one knows just what story he had in mind when he made the six tapestries, but certainly the Lady must have been a very wonderful personage. She lives always in a fairy ring; she is surrounded by animals: the most beautiful is the fabulous unicorn with his single white horn in his white forehead; the most useful and faithful is the lion. The monkey is never far away; and birds, rabbits, lambs, and even the timid fox disport themselves at the Lady's feet.

There are some, perhaps the wisest students, who say that there is no story, and that the Lady and her friends stand for the five senses: *sight* is the name of the tapestry in which the unicorn looks at his image in the mirror; *hearing*, that in which the Lady plays on a tiny portable organ; *smell*, the one where the Lady is toying with a garland of fragrant flowers, and the monkey has his nose buried in

a rose; *touch*, that in which the Lady places her hand upon the slender horn of the shy unicorn; and *taste*, that in which she is about to partake of rich fruits. The tapestry showing the Lady in front of her pavilion, where all the creatures do homage before her, is said to have been woven simply to praise her beauty and her virtues.

There is, however, an old legend that used to belong to the tapestries before scholars became as learned as they are now. It is so full of charm and so like the pictures woven by Marc that it does no harm to know it. It may serve as a beginning for the tales which every one has a right to make for himself.

The story goes something like this:

Mohammed the Second, he who conquered the great city of Constantinople, died in the year 1481. He left two sons, Bajazet and Zazim. A struggle ensued between the two, as to which one should succeed his father. War arose. Bajazet had by far the greater army at his command and was moreover much harsher and more ruthless than Zazim. Beaten and a prisoner, Zazim was forced to leave his home. Under the command of the Knights of St. John, a band of crusading princes, he was sent to France. For many months Zazim was confined in the castle of Boussac. From its high towers he looked over the fair fields of France, but they seemed cold indeed beside his memories of the blue seas of his country, the gardens shimmering in the hot sunlight, fragrant with roses and oleander.

But on a sudden, one spring morning, the fields of France became lovelier than any land he had ever known, for looking from his window, he beheld in the dewy grass beneath him the most beautiful of all maidens. Her gown was of rose-red stuff, looped over a skirt of richly figured brocade. At her throat and girdle were shining jewels, and the head-dress that covered her golden hair was jeweled also. The Lady felt his gaze upon her; and, glancing up, she saw his dark eyes sad with longing and weariness. The maiden was the Lady Blanchefort, mistress of a neighboring castle.

The Lady Blanchefort made her way to the castle of Boussac for this errand and that. It was not long before she held converse with the Turkish prince. Soon each deemed the other of more account than earth or moon or all the stars. For Zazim joy was hidden in every fold of her garments, and he dreamt of her as he had seen her that first morning with the spring flowers at her feet and all the little wood creatures enchanted by her beauty and crowding about her. So kind and so good was she that Zazim deemed that even the shy unicorn must be near; so gentle was she that he swore even the tawny lion was tamed by her smile.

The glad days of Blanchefort and the goodly prince were all too short. Zazim was sent as a prisoner to Rome. There, some say, at the order of his brother Bajazet he was poisoned. The grim deed was done, according to the old French story-tellers, by the servants of Alexandre Borgia, who was then Pope of all Christendom. The Lady Blancheforte grieved always. Soon all that was left of their joy was the flower-filled tapestries that told, so sang the old troubadours, of the Lady's beauty as she appeared to Zazim those bright mornings on the fair fields of France.

Nothing gave Pierre, Marc, and the other weavers of the Middle Ages more pleasure than the color of their tapestries. The "Perseus and Andromeda" is done in beautiful shades of tan, soft reds, and old, shadowy greens. "The Lady and the Unicorn," on the other hand, is much more gay. It is chiefly reds and blues with touches of cream and here and there faint yellows and green. The weavers loved to put into their hangings the quaint animals of which they were so fond and all the wild blossoms of their beloved countryside. Those tapestries like "The Lady and the Unicorn" series which are covered with lilies, violets, daisies, and pinks, are known to the world as *millefleurs*, or tapestries of a thousand flowers. None save the workers of the fourteenth and fifteenth centuries have made gray walls to blossom; none save these weavers have ever made millefleurs. In this they are supreme.

Sitting at their looms throughout the dark winter days, Pierre and Marc, the imaginary workers who stand for those whose very names are forgotten, sent their bobbins in and out between dull warp threads. And wherever the bobbins went, flowers bloomed, little pages danced, monkeys buried inquisitive noses in rosy petals, and fair ladies moved with stately tread. Such was the skill of the weavers of stories!

Brothers of The Quill
Illuminated Manuscripts

BROTHERS OF THE QUILL

"Look out for your fingers! Do not put them on my writing! You do not know what it is to write! It cramps your back, it obscures your eyes, it breaks your sides and stomach!" From way back in the Middle Ages comes this cry, written at the end of a beautiful manuscript made by some unknown brother of the quill. "You do not know what it is to write!" That is true. In these times of printing-presses and type-writers man does not know what it is to write; what it is to bend hour after hour over a page, the pen grasped in cramped fingers, making endless strokes, each one even, clear, correct, and beautiful. The unknown monk spoke truly. To-day we do not know what it is to write.

But they knew, these workers, who in far-away years spent their lives in the scriptoriums or writing-rooms of the monasteries. They knew all too well. One of the first things they knew about it was that time must be held as of no account. Their youth, their strength, their desires for rest, for wandering in the fields, for loitering in the woods, their fondness for eating and drinking and tale-telling were all to be held as nothing. Everything must go into the making of their books.

Since much of the book-making was done either in monasteries or by men trained by the Church, the writers might not even sign their names to the marvelous volumes when they had finished them. That was the rule of most of the orders, especially in the early part of the Middle Ages. The brothers' labor was considered to be the Lord's labor, not their own; their hands were spoken of as the servants of God. Like the weavers of stories these writers are hidden in their work. What we know of them we know chiefly through the comment, called the *Explicit*, which they were permitted to put at the end of their books. In these a little of the human side of the monk comes to light. One writer says of his undertaking: "Completed on the vigil of the Nativity of Our Lord Jesus Christ, on an empty stomach." Whether the monk had had a fast imposed upon him as a penance, or whether he thought his manu-script would be more holy if finished on an empty stomach, it is impossible to tell. But it is rather a quaint picture, that of the complaining brother, weary and feeling the pangs of hunger, who toils late on Christmas Eve to finish his required task.

One old fellow seems to have taken his work quite lightly. He wrote his *Explicit* in rhyme:

> I, Raoul Tanquy, who never was drunk
> (Or hardly more than judge or monk),
> On fourth of July finished this book,
> Then to drink at the Tabouret myself took,
> With Pylon and boon companions more,
> Who tripe and onions and garlic adore.

The writer of this was evidently not a monk, and the book upon which he was working had nothing to do with the church. It was a copy of a history written by the French Froissart. The jolly scribe toiled for his living and ate when his work was done, and that with a right good will!

If some of the monks felt overburdened or made light of their work, there were plenty who felt that it was divine. One Othlonus of Ratisbone congratulates himself, though humbly, upon his own ability: "I think proper to add an account of the knowledge and capacity for writing which was given me by the Lord in my childhood. When as yet a little child, I was sent to school and quickly learned my letters, and I began long before the time of learning and without any order from my master, to learn the art of writing. Undertaking this in a furtive and unusual manner and without any teacher, I got a habit of holding my pen wrongly, nor were any of my teachers afterward able to correct me on this point." How many like him have suffered from just such a difficulty! It brings the monk very near the modern penman.

He continues: "While in the monastery of Tergensee in Bavaria, I wrote many books. . . . Being sent to Franconia while I was yet a boy, I worked so hard that before I returned I had nearly lost my eyesight. After I became a monk at St. Emmerem, I was appointed schoolmaster. The duties of the office so fully occupied my time that I was able to do the transcribing I was interested in only by nights and in holidays. I was, however, able in addition to writing the books I had myself composed, and the copies which I gave away for the edification of those who asked for them, to prepare nineteen missals [books containing the services of the Mass for an entire year], three books of the Gospels and the Epistles, besides which I wrote four service books for Matins." Othlonus gives in addition to all these a further and much longer list of his accomplishments, ending it with the patient words: "Afterwards old age's infirmities of various kinds hindered me."

In this account of his life the good monk tells the history not of one man, but of many. A little boy with clever fingers works by himself secretly upon bits of discarded

The Letter "S." School of Bernardo Daddi, Italian, XIV Century.

parchment. He is discovered, his skill admired, his mistakes criticized, and an effort made to correct them. He is sent to school in the monastery. All schools were in monasteries then. Almost without thinking, the boy decides to become a brother himself. Nowhere in the world save within the monastic walls will he find the quiet and the peace to go on with his beloved work. In due season he becomes, himself, a teacher. He is a teacher with no evenings and no holidays. These he must spend over his beautifully written pages. The work is arduous. In time his muscles weaken; his

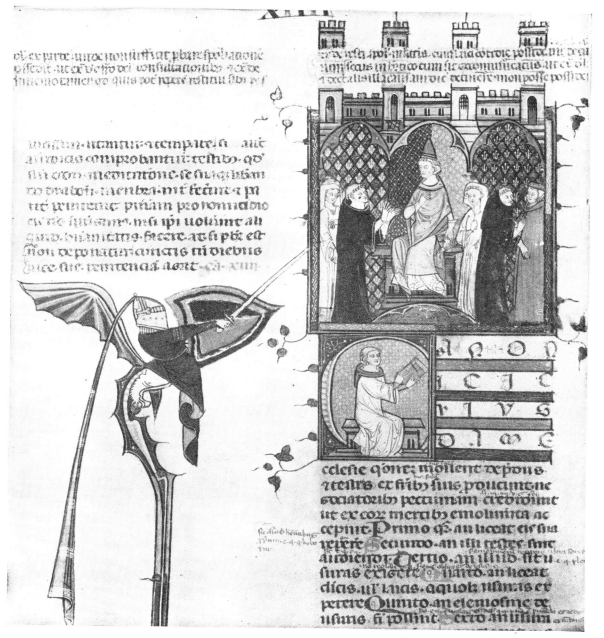

Audience Scene. English, XIV Century.

hands shake. His eyes are dimmed; the letters are no longer black and strong, but gray and far-away seeming. He must lay down his pen. "Old age's infirmities" have come upon him. Such were the lives of the brothers of the quill, hundreds and hundreds of them!

It was thought by such pious workers that the making of books brought salvation to their souls. A story is told of a worldly and frivolous brother, guilty of many sins and follies, but who, nevertheless, was an industrious scribe. When he came to die, the devil claimed his soul. The angels, however, brought before the judgment throne the great book which he had made; and for every letter therein he received pardon for one sin. Behold! When the account was completed, there proved to be one letter over! And says the story, "It was a very big book!" It is also told that in the Monastery of Maes Eych, while the illuminators were at work in the evening copying the Holy Writ, the devil in a fit of rage extinguished their candles; these, however, were promptly lighted again by a breath of the Holy Spirit, and the good work went on!

Thus the making of a book was felt to be a very important and worthy occupation, as indeed it was. Yet it may seem strange, in a time when all sorts of artificial ideas have grown up about one kind of work being "respectable" and another not, to learn that in the scale of things within the convent, scriptorium work (writing) was considered equal only to working in the fields. In the Rule of St. Fereol way back in the sixth century, there was the following sentence: "He who doth not turn up the earth with his plow ought to write parchment with his fingers."

The work of the scriptorium in a given monastery was devoted first of all to building up the library of that monastery and then to filling orders for rich patrons either within or without the Church. The monks were required not only to write but to read. This was especially true of the abbeys founded by St. Benedict. There the brothers had a regular system of lending books from the central library; and every brother was supposed to be reading some book "straight through" all the while he was at work transcribing another book. In this way the monks became real scholars and gathered ideas of what the best books should be.

The materials upon which the brothers wrote were, on the whole, very simple. They wrote chiefly upon vellum (calf's skin) and parchment (sheep's skin). This was prepared, as nearly as one can find out, by washing the skin, letting it lie in a lime solution for three days, washing a second time, stretching evenly on a frame, scraping once more and paring down inequalities in the surface. Then the parchment was dusted with sifted chalk and rubbed with pumice. Despite all this care there seems to have been a slight difference between the skin side and the hairy side; and when the book was bound, it was so arranged that hairy side was opposite hairy side, skin side opposite skin side. This was done, of course, so that when the two pages lay open, they would be uniform in texture.

The Annunciation. Italian, First Half of the XV Century.

The early manuscripts were written in black and occasionally in silver or gold inks. As time went on, the initial letter of each page began to assume greater and greater importance. Colors were used to beautify it and often a great deal of gold. Still later, the initial letter gave way to pictures, small in size, occupying the place the initial letter had formerly held on the page. Red was a very popular color in these pictures; it was called *minium*; the artist who applied it was called *mineator*; the pictures themselves, miniatures. Later the word was used for any picture of a small size.

Apparently one of the difficulties the monks had was that of making the gold stick to the vellum or parchment. Many rather absurd recipes have been handed down. They are more amusing than useful. One such rule directs the illuminator to make a simple paste from incense, white gum, and sugar candy, distempering it with wine. Another suggests the white of an egg whipped in the milk of a fig tree and powdered gum arabic. Gum and rose water is also prescribed, as are honey and again white of egg. Still another formula is written: " . . . cut up thick parchment or vellum . . . wash and cook it. Prepare also the skin of an eel carefully scraped, cut up and washed in the same manner. Prepare thus also the bones of the head of the wolf-fish washed and dried. To whichever of these you have prepared add a third part of very transparent gum, simmer it a little, and you can keep it as long as you wish."

These pastes were to be laid upon the initial letter or upon the background of the miniature, and upon them the gold was to be applied. It was supposed to stick. Modern experimenters report, however, that none of these suggestions prove practical and the gold slides neatly off the parchment! Probably the secret was the skill of individual workers combined with almost any sticky substance. Men whose skill was equal to the difficulties left their rules, which are of no use to those not versed in the old practices.

The colors used by the brothers were made from herbs and chemicals often mixed in the monastery itself. In those days the doctor, or leech as he was often called, had a wide knowledge of herbs and medicines gained through his practice. This was useful to the artist in the preparation of his paints. The various colors were commonly preserved by steeping small pieces of linen in the tinted extracts. An old manuscript says of the process: "When the aforesaid pieces are dry, put them in a book of cotton paper, and keep the book under your pillow that it may take no damp; and when you want to use the colors, cut off a small portion (of the cloth) and place it in a shell with a little water the evening before. In the morning the tint will be

Troy Town. French, Late XV or Early XVI Century.

ready, the color being extracted from the linen." Shells, it seems, were used by the monks as little cups in which to mix their different colors.

An old recipe for black ink directs you to "cut for yourself wood of the thorn-trees in April or in May, before they produce flowers or leaves, and collecting them in small bundles, allow them to lie in the shade for two or three or four weeks until they are dry." Then you are to beat off the bark, put it into a barrel full of water which must be allowed to stand for eight days until the water "imbibes all the sap of the bark. Afterward put the water into a clean pan and boil it. This must be done many times until at last much of the water has boiled away and the mixture begins to blacken and cook until a sort of skin forms upon the surface. When you see this, take the pot from the fire and let the mixture sit in the sun until the black ink purifies itself from the red dregs. Afterward take small bags of parchment care-fully sewn . . . and pouring in the pure ink, suspend them in the sun until all is quite dry; and when dry take from the bags as much (powder) as you wish, and temper it with wine over the fire, and, adding a little vitriol, write."

Gold was ground in a little mortar or dish with a small pestle or hammer. The preparation of this was a very lengthy task, much lengthier even than the making of ink. When the gold was ground, it was mixed with pure minium (red lead) and a "third part cinnabar" (vermilion). The solution was then put through a most elaborate process of mixing, grinding, and washing, and was finally applied to a letter or a miniature with one of the strange glues. When the gold had dried, it was polished with a "hound's tooth or a bloodstone upon a shining horn tablet." Then it gleamed forth boldly—unless too much paste had been used, when oh, sad to say, it black-ened and would not receive its polish.

That the mere getting ready to write was no small undertaking, it is easy to see. Then came the real task: the patient forming of each letter; the delicate lines of the initial; or the even more difficult work upon the miniature. Occasionally one man did all these things, but rarely. In some cases the materials were bought by those abbeys which were rich enough. If this was not possible, the preparation of inks and colors, parchment and vellum, was done by one group of monks; the writing was done by a brother versed in that art; the initials were made by a second; the miniature by a third; the binding by perhaps a fourth and a fifth brother. For the process of binding a book was in itself a very long one. The books were some-times bound in heavy calfskin tanned with sumac, alum, and oak bark. Sometimes the bindings were of velvet, sometimes of metal work decorated with ivory, enamel, or precious jewels. The clasps which fastened the great books were of the finest work of the goldsmith. It was little wonder that the precious volumes were often chained in their places.

Among the most popular books were the Books of Hours, which contained a text for each hour of the day. These were especial favorites of the ladies of the court. A French poet writes of a lady's desire for one of these:

> Hours of Our Lady should be mine,
> Fitting for a noble dame
> Of lofty lineage and name;
> Wrought most cunningly and quaint
> In richest gold and azure paint.
> Rare covering of cloth of gold
> Full daintily it shall enfold,
> Or, open to the view exposed,
> Two golden clasps to keep it closed.

Such books were gifts fit for queen or prince, and were coveted by the most powerful. A description of them does very little to bring any idea of their beauty before the mind. Even reproductions of the pages are unsatisfactory because the color of initial and miniature forms one of their chiefest attractions. But at least a reproduction does give an idea of the lovely forms and of the great care that has been exercised by scribes. The illustration of the initial shows how charmingly the makers of books decorated this most important part of the page. "The Audience Scene" makes very clear the way in which the miniatures were worked into the design of the whole page. The knight with the tail of a dragon tells that the brothers of the quill who made this page joke along with the rest of the world. Knights were always swaggering and boasting to the folk how much greater the sword was than the pen. The brother smiled to himself, thinking how bright his work would be when the swords were rusty and forgotten; and to pay the knights for their vaunts, he gave them the forms of beasts. Knights were not the only ones to suffer at the hands of the illuminators. A certain bishop, overly strict with his rules, was always listening to tales of wrongdoing; an abbot was too slow at his prayers; a priest was too fond of his victuals. Behold in some old manuscript a bishop with the long ears of a rabbit, an abbot with cobwebs growing from his hat, or a priest with a leg of mutton in his hand instead of his staff.

The miniature of "Medusa" shows the maiden and her attendants before she had tried to vie in beauty with Athena and had been turned into the Gorgon, a monster with snaky locks. The illuminators of manuscripts, like the weavers of stories, dressed characters from Greek mythology in the costumes of their own Middle

Ages. Strangely enough, in the background, two servitors of Medusa may be seen engaged in a joust such as the knights of European courts enjoyed.

Another illumination having to do with a classical subject is "Troy Town." Looking at the town, the reader would certainly guess it to be some thriving French city of the Middle Ages, perhaps Paris itself. Here again the worker of medieval times sees all scenes and places as he sees his own. There in Troy, where the Greeks fought to win back the fair Helen, is a shoe and hat shop, where good French citizens of the late fourteen or early fifteen hundreds did their shopping. Beneath the arch a

Medusa Enthroned as Queen. French, School of Tours, Second Half of the XV Century.

[28]

chemist is pounding in his mortar with a pestle, preparing, perhaps, some strange concoction for an alchemist who sought to make gold. French workmen labor on the tower and stroll about the streets of the ancient city.

This Troy Town is a place of riddles indeed, only to be explained by the fact that from the twelfth century downward many famous romances were written about Troy by writers who knew little or nothing of the old Greek sources. They wrote chiefly from tales gathered out of old manuscripts, none too accurate, and added to by their own imaginations. The stories they told were French, having but a slight connection with Greek war songs and the great blind bard.

"The Annunciation," in which the angel kneels before the Virgin, telling her that she is to become the mother of the Child Jesus, is exquisite with signs of how the brothers loved the flowers and the beasts of the field. Little bunnies hop about; a dove flies near. The trees blossom with little golden blooms, and the grass grows thickly beneath Our Lady's feet. All day long the miniaturist worked in the gray writing-room, but he looked out upon spring advancing over the fair Italian hills. Some of it entered his brush. He made his page a fitting place for spring— even spring in Italy—to rest her silver heel.

One John Skelton, poet, and tutor to King Henry VIII of England, writes quaintly of the books of his day. Three or four words, no longer in use, may be slightly puzzling: *bice* is a blue or green pigment; *lozende* means diamond-shaped; *railes*, probably just lines; *englozed with* is the same as glazed or made shining.

> With that of boke lozende were the clasps,
> The margin was illumined with golden railes,
> And bice empictured, with grasshoppers and waspes
> And butterflies and fresh peacocks' tailes:
> Englozed with pictures well touched and quickly,
> It wold have made a man hole that had right to be sickly.

What more can be said of the work of the brothers of the quill? A poor monk cried out, "Do not put your fingers on my writing," and describes the pain he had in completing his book. And yet just to look at its bright pages is enough to "make a man hole that had right to be sickly."

Wood-Carvers
of Long Ago

WOOD-CARVERS OF LONG AGO

Bending under his load of mortar, a priest might be seen walking through a great open space filled with timbers and gigantic piles of stones for the building of a church. He felt himself not humbled by the task, but rather uplifted. In the old days, in the Middle Ages, the great churches were built by half the town; and all the country round watched the rearing of the cathedral, talked it, planned for it. While a priest or even a bishop wrestled with his heavy load, high above him some poor workman with no learning, but with skill in his fingers, would be carving a leaf or scroll pattern on a column. He who served, served as best he could. A bishop might take but a lowly place while the carver seemed very important. That was because no one thought of himself, but only of the church that was being built for the Virgin.

Since the church was built not for the honor of man, but for the glory of Our Lady, it was not necessary that any one should know who made this statue or that carven archway. Like the weavers and illuminators, the wood-carvers were simple craftsmen most of whose names have not come down to us. More than either of the other two bodies of artists, they worked in large groups. All labored together for their church. They were often known by their group names, as the "wood-carvers of Lille," "the carvers of the choir stall of Amiens," or "the carvers of the altar at Rouen."

A Russian Toy in the Making.

[32]

Very often the craft of wood-carving was a thing handed down from father to son so that the children used the hard block and sharp knives with absolute naturalness. A boy, as he was growing up, would be known as Jean, the wood-carver's son; then later when his fingers stiffened a bit, he would be known as Jean, the father of Pierre the wood-carver; and when he grew quite old, as the grandfather of Michel who carves in wood; and then later, perhaps, even as the great-grandfather of tiny Joseph, who was already beginning to play with sticks of wood and to cut his small thumbs as well as the wood. So it went. Little wonder that these men could make branches of dead trees seem to put forth new leaves and grow young again; that they could turn a gnarled root into a grinning face or a strange animal.

Like the weavers, the wood-carvers also had their guilds. The rules were very strict, and the young apprentice had an anxious time when his seven years of service was over and the time had come for him to prove himself worthy to become a master. This he did by making some object which should meet the standard of the guild. He was judged by keen-eyed men who could see any flaw and any hesitation at a glance.

The young apprentice and his masters worked just as men do to-day. The ways of carving have not changed. Perhaps the illustration of a toy made by a modern Russian peasant will show better than any description how a dull block of wood can be changed under a skillful knife. Our fifteenth-century wood-carver labored just as did this Russian villager, only, in most instances, more seriously. He first chiseled out the broad planes and surfaces; then gradually with infinite patience he cut here a lock of hair, there a smile, until after weeks or perhaps months of work the thing was done. The clear thinking and the controlled muscles of the worker showed in every curve. The little statue of the mourning Virgin is

A Russian Toy in the Making.

[33]

an excellent example of the fine craftsmanship and the deep sincerity of these early carvers.

The Madonna wears a blue robe and a rose-colored gown, which have been touched by the kindly hand of time until the hues seem not colors but rather memories of colors. Little is known about her beyond the fact that she was carved somewhere in France sometime during the fourteen hundreds; and that she was one of a group made up of those mourning about the body of Christ. Such groups, or *pietàs* as they were called, were brought out into the churches only at a certain time of the year, the time when the Good Friday mass was sung; just as at Christmas time there appeared on the altars marvelously lifelike wooden figures gathered about the manger to worship the Child.

The maker of this figure, Jean, Pierre, Michel—no one knows—lived probably in a very simple house on a queer, dark, twisting, ill-paved street that resounded all day with stiff peasant carts and the hoofs of horses clattering across badly laid cobblestones, while the horses' owners shouted and hooted to hasten their beasts and reach the market before an equally eager neighbor succeeded in so doing. But though the street was narrow and not too clean, the house itself was undoubtedly very charming and showed in every corner what craft its owner followed. Gates, gateposts, doors, were carved; fireplaces and chairs, beds, tables, even bobbins which the women used in lacemaking, and spinning wheels, showed what a clever knife was here. Often, as in the case of the Virgin, color was put upon the wood after it was carved. The colors were few and simple, and often, one imagines, made at home.

Not only were houses carved, but also shops. Not only those of the carver, but those of other craftsmen were beautifully decorated. Compare the modern shoe, clothing, grocery store with the armorer's shop illustrated in the next chapter. Skilled workmanship went hand in hand with everyday industry, with buying and selling. Marketing in the days of the fifteenth-century wood-carver was often done under roofs that to-day might well be used for the finest dwelling or church.

Knowing something of the conditions under which the artists worked helps us to understand such a figure as that of the Virgin. And yet to look at her and remember that once there lay before her creator only a log of well-selected wood takes almost more imagination than the modern mind possesses.

Quite as remarkable in its way is the abbot's stall. The stall—a name often given to the throne of a king or of a church dignitary—is the work of a master craftsman who lived in the early sixteenth century. Certain of the stalls in churches

The Mourning Virgin. French, XV Century.

and monasteries were reserved for great personages and accordingly were very richly decorated. On the upright above the right arm of the canopied seat is a shield, the heraldry of which shows the stall to have been the seat of an abbot.

The abbot's seat is elevated above the bench beside it. That was a constant reminder that in the life of the monastery the abbot was lord over all the monks and lay brothers. On the lower seat sat the scribe, who, bent over his scroll of parchment, was accustomed to take down the word of his master as the abbot dictated the rules and charters of his institution. The pinnacles on the canopy are pointed, top and bottom, not only because their form adds to the great delicacy and charm of the carving, but because they stand as a symbol of the dual power of the abbot. He was the great dignitary of his order and at the same time a powerful feudal *seigneur* with control, often, over vast lands and many houses.

The back of the abbot's seat is decorated by a theme which was very popular with the artists of the Middle Ages—the Jesse tree. The Jesse tree is the genealogical or "family tree" of Christ. It refers to a prophecy in Isaiah which foretold that the great Saviour should come of the line of David, the son of Jesse. The Jesse tree on the back of the abbot's seat has the kings and princes of the line of David perched in the branches of a great beech or ash. It is interesting to note that all of these folk are in the costume of the fifteenth century. The wood-carvers, like the tapestry weavers, thought of their heroes as wearing a garb like their own. One of the most fascinating things about the Jesse tree is that it still retains unmistakable traces of the brilliant colors in which it was originally painted.

In the angles on each side of the arch which forms the top of the panel containing the Jesse tree are two figures, at the right a shepherd with his crook, at the left a woman plying her distaff. These symbolize the fact that the abbot is both shepherd of his flock and manager of his monastic house. The lower part of the back beneath the Jesse tree contains a panel upon which is an interesting portrait in relief between flower designs and two of the grotesque animal heads of which the craftsmen of the day were so fond. Perhaps the wood-carver had been a soldier in Italy, where he had seen doors, altars, and benches decorated with just such strange beasts, portraits, and cleverly interwoven garlands. Charmed, he may have brought memories of them home with him. Anyway it was through soldiering and other more peaceful means of travel that, about 1500, Italian ideas were finding their way into the minds of Frenchmen.

Besides such beautiful objects as the Virgin and the abbot's stall, both carved with a religious purpose and serious intent, the wood-carver of the Middle Ages

An Abbot's Stall. French, 1500-1515.

also liked his jokes, his tales of peasant folk and of animals. Many of these are to be found tucked away in *misericords* or "indulgence seats" of the churches. Those which are illustrated are all English. It was an early rule of the Church that every one, save the sick or old and infirm, had to stand throughout all the long, long services. This was really a great trial of strength and a cause for much lamenting. Finally seats on pivots were put into the churches. These seats could be moved up and down like those in our theaters. On the bottom of the seats there were little ledges made so that when the seat folded up, the worshiper could at least have the comfort of leaning against something firm. Such seats were placed first of all, and most often, in the choir-stalls for the monks and canons. But later they were also given at times to those members of the congregation who were least able to endure the long services. In many cases the ledges of the misericords were delightfully carved.

The wood-carver had much to do in the churches. There were the altar screens, and the great lectern, which held the Bible and to which it was often chained. Beams and arches, columns and doors were enlivened by his hand. From all these marvelous objects the little ledges of the misericords have been chosen for illustration and discussion because they show so clearly the everyday life of the people of the Middle Ages. For beneath these ledges the carver felt free to carve not only religious subjects, but common things. Here he even carved his "funnies." Here he felt secure from the prying eyes of priest and bishop.

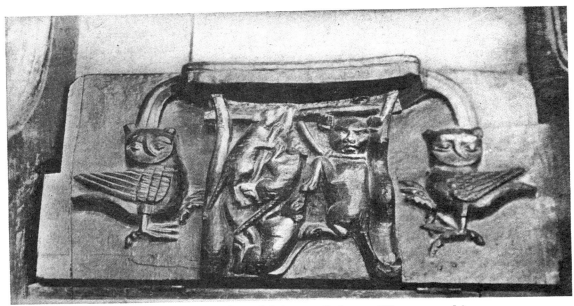

Rats Hanging a Cat. Malvern Priory, Worcestershire.

That he was not entirely safe, however, is shown by the sharp questionings of St. Bernard of Clairvaux, writing to William, Abbot of St. Thierry, in 1125: "What mean those ridiculous monstrosities in the courts of cloisters; those filthy apes, those fierce lions, those monstrous centaurs, those half-men, those spotted tigers, those fighting soldiers, and horn-blowing hunters; many bodies attached under one head or many heads to one body; here a serpent's tail attached to a quadruped, there a quadruped's head on a fish; here a beast presenting the fore parts of a horse, and dragging after it the rear of a goat; there a horned animal with the hind parts of a horse?"

What meant they indeed? Sometimes they were for the amusement of the carver and onlooker; sometimes they were merely pictures of the everyday occupations of the folk; and often they were in all seriousness a record of the natural sciences as the common folk knew them.

The knowledge of animals which the people of the Middle Ages had, came largely from a book called the "Physiologus." This was a mighty medieval tome based on a work of Pliny, an ancient Roman scholar. The man of the twelfth or thirteenth century took what he had learned from Pliny about animals, joined with this Bible texts, and so made the various creatures serve to illustrate moral lessons. The lessons may have been much needed, but the facts about animals were

The Lion. Malvern Priory, Worcestershire.

sometimes wondrous strange. Most of the folk learned their "Physiologus" not from reading it, but from stories from it told in paint, in weaving, in stone, glass, or wood.

Of the lion, for instance, says the "Physiologus": "He has three natures: first he wipes away the marks of his footprints with his tail so that none can follow him; second, he sleeps with his eyes open, always on the alert for his prey; third, he has a monstrous loud roar." The lion is often carved on the portals of churches as a guardian of the sanctuary.

"The nature of the antelope is that it has two powerful horns with which it saws through trees and fells them. It is especially easy to catch the antelope along the banks of the Euphrates River; there grow shrubs of pleasant savor very agreeable to the antelope. If the antelope gets his horns entangled in their branches, the hunter can come up and kill him with little or no difficulty." The moral of this, says the "Physiologus," is that the Christian who allows himself to become entangled in the thickets of avarice, pride, and all other evil passions falls an easy prey to the devil.

Stranger even than tales of real creatures are those of imaginary ones. The *griffin* is a beast with the head and wings of a bird and the body of a lion. He is said to be so strong that he can fly away with a full-grown ox. Then there is the *tharanda*, which has the shape of the ox and the fur of the bear and changes color

The Antelope. Chapel of Canon Pyon, Herefordshire.

[40]

like the chameleon, while the terrible man-eating *manticora* has the face of a man, the eyes and mane of a lion, a scorpion's tail, and the flight of an eagle.

Often the scenes on the misericords are simply representations of the everyday life which the carver knew so well. There is the Packman. He was the traveling store. And indeed in those days it was necessary that the store should travel. The roads were bad; often they led through dark forests inhabited by robbers and bandits and wild beasts. Besides, the goodwife could not go to town or to the fair merely for the wanting. She had to wait until the master could leave his woodcutting or his crops. He would then saddle his horse and take her behind him on a pillion. Even then the path was not too safe; certainly it was not an easy one. So the traveling store was a great boon. The Packman had to be a hardy fellow. He carried a heavy stave and doggedly made his way from castle to village, from hostelry to cottage.

Complaint was lodged with the bishops more than once because the Packman displayed his wares in the porch of the church on Sunday. This seems indeed an outrageous thing, but in those days the gray Puritan fathers had not laid down their strict laws as to how the Sabbath should be kept. And what could be more delightful to a housewife, isolated by her own fireside perhaps for many weeks, than to gossip with her friends over the contents of the peddler's box? Since the Packman opened his wares, at times, before the very doors of the church, it does

Pruning, April. Malvern Priory, Worcestershire.

[41]

not seem strange to see him grinning out from under the ledge of an "indulgence seat," a misericord.

The illuminations in a quaint old manuscript of the late thirteenth century tell what eager dames were likely to find in his pack. In the minatures, a Pack-man has fallen asleep under a tree. While he is napping, some mischievous monkeys discover his box and open it. One of them has pulled off the wrapper, and others are running away with the contents; a man's shirt can be seen and some circular mirrors. A number of apes have climbed a tree, and you can make out a purse and a belt, a musical pipe, a sheath and dagger, a pair of slippers, hood and gloves, and a large mirror, A continuation of the story shows the inquisitive creatures playing with a man's hat, a woman's kerchief, hose, a woman's head-dress, and a man's hood. This strange tale shows quite clearly what was to be found in the peddler's pack.

But more important than any or all of these articles to the lonely housewife was the gossip the Packman brought. He was the newspaper of the day. Whole villages hung eagerly upon his slightest word. And what tales he told, what marvels he saw—mostly when he was alone upon the road and had plenty of time in which to concoct them!

Besides the Packman the months of the year were popular subjects with the carvers of misericords, and in these they often pictured the everyday duties of the farmer. Winter, says an old proverb, is

No season for hedge;
Get beetle and wedge;
Cleave logs now all
For kitchen and hall.

So in "February" at Ripple Church the Goodman and his wife sit close by the fire over the pot. Apparently the master has heeded the proverb well; with great wooden hammer, or beetle, and with wedge he has split oak, beech, and aspen for his hearth. Winds may blow; snow may cover barnyard and field; but the two are warm within. 'Tis true the master has a cold in his head and wears gloves; while the mistress spins, the cat sits upon her chairback for added comfort as it gravely washes its paws.

"King Sol," the sun of course, might very likely be called "March" as well, for March is represented in an early third-century calendar by a full-faced sun, and in more than one misericord, he stands as the symbol of that month. At

The Scold.

The Packman.
Two Misericords from Ludlow Church, Shropshire.

All Saints' Church, Hereford, he certainly appears in full glory, crowned like the ruling monarch he is. He's a bit of a wag, too, with his wide grin; and his children on each side of him, the daisies, seem anything but "modest and shy" as poets would have us think them. They look very much as if they had had a little too much dew to drink and were still wishing and plotting for more.

"April—Bird Scaring" shows two hardy countrymen with sticks, beating the air and howling to keep the thieving fowls away from crops which have been planted with so much labor. It is worth while to note their costume, the long hosen and the simple jerkin with wide sleeves. "April" from Malvern Priory, shows the farmer pruning some early growth. The birds on each side suggest the return of spring, as does his occupation. It is interesting to see that the pruning shears are quite modern in their form.

From Hereford, All Saints' Church, comes a jovial fellow, "Mr. Nobody," or perhaps better "The Contortionist." He shows the folk not at work, but at play. Among the villagers and commoners of the town, the stately dances of the court were not in the least the fashion. The worthies in country parishes preferred to see dancing bears and monkeys, strange women from eastern lands who could stand on their heads or turn a somersault. Tumblers were well liked; and contortionists, those who could take absurd and twisted poses, "turn themselves inside out," were much in vogue. That is why this wight smiles so broadly; he is sure of a welcome wherever there is a crowd.

These same village folk loved, too, their topsy-turvy world. Misericords are seen in which the goodman literally drives the cart before the horse. A rider sits in the saddle facing his nag's tail. The weaker are given victory over the strong: a rabbit has a bit in the mouth of the fox and is riding him just as in Uncle Remus's story of "Brer Rabbit"; a monkey is astride a cat and combs its back with a large comb. At Malvern three mice who have long been harried by the house cat have brought Mr. Tom to justice and are hanging him to the limb of a tree.

But no one must think that all carvings of this time are without their moral lessons. Quite the contrary. A miser is counting his gold at Beverly Minster, but down below lurks the devil on the point of seizing him. Stealing butter and cream was the cardinal sin among the farming folk; no one with any trace of humanity would stoop to such a crime, so at one of the choir-stalls of Lincoln Minster, it is a beast, an ape, who runs away with the goodwife's churnings. Gossip, at least too much of it, was also a sin; and a village scold was never too popular. It was she who complained of all mischievous small boys; it was she who told this evil

King Sol.

Mr. Nobody.

Two Misericords from All Saints' Church, Hereford

tale and listened to that. She was always belittling, chiding, or denouncing a poor victim. At last the folk got tired of her. In some villages they ducked her in the pond; in others they gagged her. At Ludlow Church she is to be seen in the latter state.

It is just because they do tell us of the daily pranks, dreams, duties, and pleasures of a medieval village that these misericords are so valuable. If you try at all, it is not hard to find out about kings and princes, bishops and popes, saints and scoundrels of any historical period; but to learn about the common folk is not so easy. It is the President who has his photograph in the paper every morning, not the man who sells vegetables, buys rags and old paper, or delivers coal. So it has always been.

After all, it is the *folk* who make up the life of any land; if you do not know them, you do not know the country or the age.

Still it is not chiefly as records that these carvings bid the traveler to stop and look. They are full of vigor and truth both as to form and as to the spirit in which they were done. Hidden away in the dark beneath the seats of the church or chapel is found some of the most original and honest work done in any time and place, however great and important.

Bird Scaring, April.

Man and Woman at Fireside, February.
Two Misericords from Ripple Church, Worcestershire.

The Armorer

ST. ELIGIVS

THE ARMORER

The craft of the armorer goes back so far into the beginnings of things that no one can trace it; it is almost as old as history. In the very early days, the armorer and the blacksmith were often one. This was true even of St. Eligius, the patron saint of armorers. Indeed, Eligius is said to have labored as a young man at the triple trade of goldsmith, blacksmith, and armorer. One day he would make a beautiful gold or silver vessel for the church; the next day he would struggle mightily in the forging of a sword; and on the third day he would give some steed a new pair of shoes. Once while he was at work upon a shrine for a church—so the old story goes— there was a rush of hot wind, a stamping of hoofs, a smell of fire and brimstone. Lo, enveloped in clouds of smoke, the devil stood before the anvil of St. Eligius. He had come to tempt him. Quick as a wink Eligius seized the devil's nose with red-hot tongs. That was the last visit the devil ever made to the saint!

Another day a very frisky horse was brought to him. The horse stamped and reared and would not allow himself to be shod. With no hesitation whatsoever St. Eligius took off the horse's leg, put the shoe on his hoof, returned the leg to the horse, which galloped off as though nothing had happened. Some say it was because of these miracles that Eligius was made bishop of the Church and patron saint of the Armorers' Guild. Others say it was because he was such an excellent craftsman and served so well his king, Clotaire II, who lived in the very early days of Paris, in 586-629. This much is certain: he would never have been chosen by all the workers in metal to represent them had he not been an excellent workman himself.

As time went on, the work of the armorer became divided. One man would spend all his time as a blacksmith; another would become a goldsmith and work only with precious metals; a third would spend his days making strong helmets and suits of mail. The exact time* at which the armorer learned to make mail, chain armor, is somewhat difficult to discover; but we say in a very general way that the Normans began to be clothed in a kind of mail about the year 800 A. D., that is to say, about two hundred and fifty years before William the Conqueror fought the battle of Hastings. By 1250 the knight was in full chain armor, and half a century later he had begun to change from mail to plate. By 1350 he was in full plate; and this he wore until about 1580, when armor got so heavy that he preferred to fight without it or at least with less of it. In the time of St. Eligius the knights wore padded leather jackets; but they did have helmets made of metal; they did have swords, of course, and spears, and thongs studded with metal knobs, which were wound around their legs.

The armorer's task will here be considered first in the period of chain mail. In the beginning of this period he had no means even of drawing the wire from which the separate links were made. Starting with a small bar of iron, the armorer heated and hammered until the metal was like fine wire. This he wound around a small circular stake so that the wire assumed the desired shape, a circle. He cut these small circles into links; the ends of each one he flattened, pierced, and fastened together with a tiny nail or, more correctly, rivet. Often these rivets were no larger than the head of a pin. When one link had its ends riveted together, another was put through it and fastened in the same way. Thus link by link the shirt was made. One shirt in a certain museum, a shirt having rather coarse links, is estimated to contain a hundred thousand of them! As the shirt of mail was but a small part of the knight's costume, it is easy to see what a gigantic piece of work the armorer had to do. The equipping of a knight in a full suit of chain mail was often a matter of months.

* Dates taken from "Helmets and Body Armor in Modern Warfare," Bashford Dean, Ph.D.

At this time there were not only armorers who dealt in metal, but, strange to say, there were also "linen armorers" who equipped the knights with suits which they wore under their mail, and with the heavily padded caps which they wore under their helms. The suits were wadded with cotton, tow, and sometimes bits of horn or

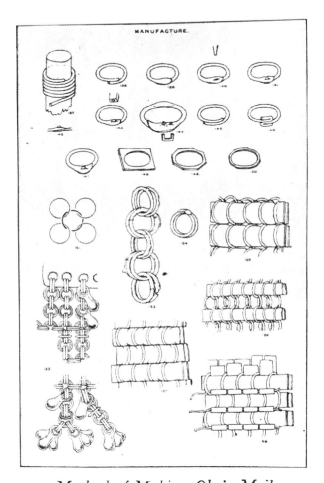

Method of Making Chain Mail.

After de Cosson, *Helmets and Examples of Mail*, London, 1880.

mail. Cloth was also used in the knight's costume for the rich cloaks worn over the armor.

The question of protecting the knight was only part of the armorer's duty. He had also to provide the knight with offensive arms such as swords, lances, crossbows, maces, and war hammers as well as various kinds of weapons put on long shafts and

Bascinet, Hauberk, and Sword. Italian, XIV Century.

called pole arms. Many of these are very strange in shape and have strange names, as for instance, the "morning star." The "morning star" is a big iron ball with long spikes in it; the ball is attached to a long pole. Perhaps it is called the "morning star" because the spikes suggest the rays of the star when it is first dimly seen, perhaps because it made the knight who was hit with it "see stars," as well it might. Rather closely related to this weapon, though on a short handle, is the "holy water sprinkler," a cruel iron ball which swings on a long iron chain. This may have sug-

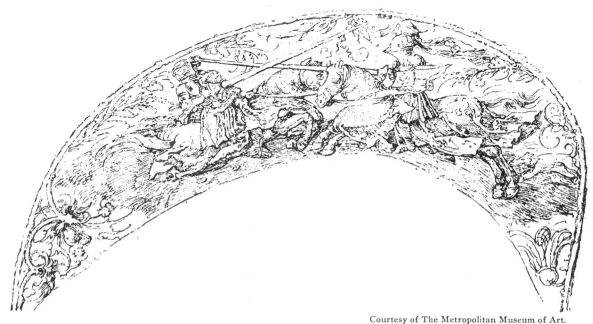

Courtesy of The Metropolitan Museum of Art.

Design for Armor, by Albrecht Dürer.

gested the little perforated ball used for sprinkling the altars in churches with water that had been blessed.

Even more unusual is a much later weapon, the Venetian feather-staff. This looks like the ordinary long staff or cane with which the gentlemen of Venice used to steady themselves when walking over the cobbled quays of their native city. But give the cane a sudden forward movement and out of a secret fastening at the top come three shining blades, sharp, death-dealing feathers. These and many more curious devices, the armorer had to work out for the safety of his man.

In truth the history of armor and of the craft of the armorer is rather like a race between the makers of weapons and the makers of defense armor. Some man would invent a new kind of weapon. His rival, across the court or in another country, would

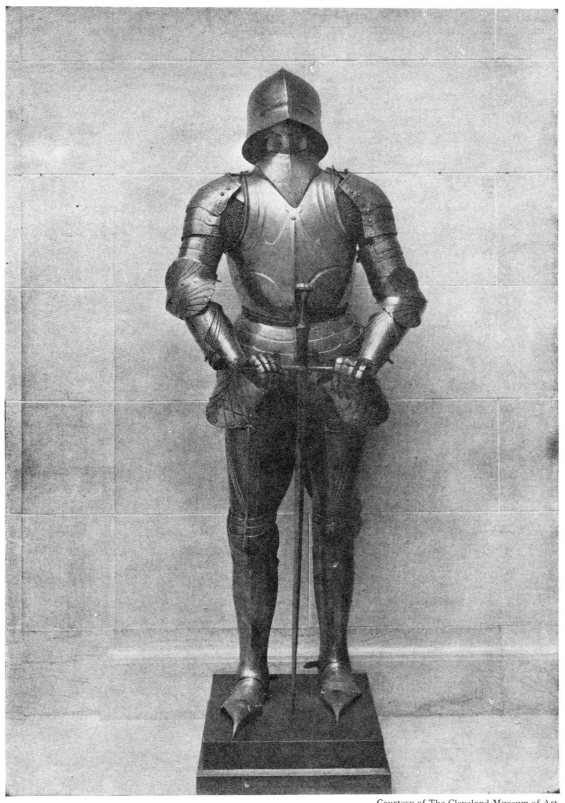

Suit of Gothic Armor. About 1480.

invent a new kind of armor to protect the knight from that weapon. Whereupon a third armorer would hammer out a weapon that would crush the new armor, and so it went. The early guns made but slight impression in the race just at the beginning, but in the end they won it. It is amusing to realize of how little use they seemed when they were first invented. The writer knows of a tiny revolver fastened to a great sword blade. If the revolver didn't work, and it usually didn't, the warrior could thrust with his sword. A gun which the writer also knows has a muzzle made

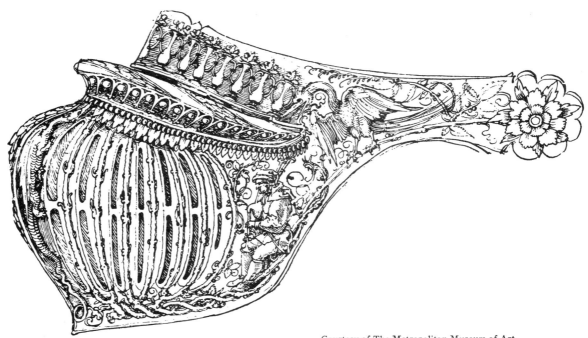

Courtesy of The Metropolitan Museum of Art.
Design for Armor, by Albrecht Dürer.

in the shape of a mace or war club. If the gun failed to go off, and this frequently happened, the user of the weapon could swing the mace.

But the time came, and quickly, when such arrangements were no longer necessary. The gun became more and more deadly, and the armor had to be made so heavy that, by the latter part of the fifteen hundreds, armor as we knew it in the early Middle Ages was no longer worn. The great armor period was drawing near its close. Modern times were beginning. They began first of all with armor which covered only the most important parts of the body, the three-quarter harness. They continued in Colonial times when even less armor was used. And in the great World War all that most of us knew about was the Tommy's or Yankee's "tin hat." With

Courtesy of The Cleveland Museum of Art.

Suit of Maximilian Armor. Early XVI Century.

the ending of the sixteen hundreds the armorer as a great craftsman was no longer known.

His best days perhaps were in the fourteen hundreds, when he made what we know as Gothic armor. In those times churches were being built with high and slender spires; doorways and windows were high and pointed, and the statues that decorated these churches were slim and tall. The costume of the day also reflected this length of line. Long, flowing garments were worn, which had long and flowing sleeves. Shoes were long and pointed like the tips of the arched windows or the church spires. In, fact, they were so pointed and so long that princes and even little pages had to wear chains or cords on the ends of their shoes to hold the toes up and keep themselves from tripping.

Gothic armor followed the same general style as the clothes which the gentlemen were wearing. The armorer had not only to protect his knight, make his armor beautiful to behold, but he had to see that it was well in the forefront of fashion. The illustration of Gothic armor shows the long pointed shoes, long points on gloves, or gauntlets, and the lower part of the breastplate formed in points quite like the spire of a church. The whole effect of the armor is slender but not exaggerated. It follows very closely the natural lines of the human figure. It depends for its beauty not on surface decoration so much as on the smooth, clean, finely burnished, and warlike surfaces.

Even the sword worn with Gothic armor was very slender. It had begun to show a curve at the hilt. The earlier swords were almost as plain as those which small boys carve from wood, with straight, rather wide blades, straight crosspieces, simple handles. As the centuries progressed, the swords grew more slender, and their pommels and hand-guards became more and more elaborate, until we come down to the rapiers with their blades both tough and flexible, and their handles as lovely as jewels.

The tendency toward greater decorativeness showed very cleverly in what is known as Maximilian armor. This kind of armor was named after a great emperor of the Holy Roman Empire, the empire of the Germanic peoples. Through his second wife, Bianca Sforza, daughter of the Duke of Milan, in Italy, Maximilian gained control of Milan. This duchy at that time gave the law in all matters of dress, as our word "milliner" clearly shows. Maximilian introduced the Milanese style into Italy and worked out the new type of armor with the help of his famous armorers, the Seusenhofers. One of its distinguishing marks is the fluting, the up-and-down ridges that may be seen all over the suits. Many fine suits, though without fluting, were given by Maximilian to his friend, King Henry VIII of England; many wonderful suits were received by him in turn from the father of Elizabeth.

Both monarchs were very enthusiastic about the two most popular sports of the time: the joust, which was a combat of strength between two knights; the tourna-

Courtesy of The Cleveland Museum of Art.

A Colletin (neck defense). French, XVI Century.

ment, which was a combat between many knights ranged on two sides like the opposing teams of a baseball or football game. A number of the suits of armor belonging to these two rulers were suits made especially for the joust or the tournament. This usually meant an outfit for both man and horse. The armorer had to

[59]

protect the steeds of the day as well as the princes who rode them. Like Gothic armor the Maximilian war harness followed the fashion of the day. At this time men were wearing full doublets with wide puffed sleeves, long hosen, and great wide-toed shoes. The illustration of Maximilian armor shows how it followed the general lines of such a costume.

The plates of a suit of armor, whether Gothic, Maximilian, or the later so-called decorated armor, were all of them hammered out over variously shaped stakes. These stakes were of iron fastened very securely in a wooden base. Sometimes they were slightly rounded to help in forming the gentle curve of a shoulder-piece; sometimes they were sharply pointed to help in the making of a helmet. Stakes were large and small, heavy and light. A great many of them were needed for a single suit. In addition to the stakes the armorer often had recourse to his anvil.

One of the things to which the maker of plate armor had to give especial consideration was the glancing or sliding surface. He had to form his surfaces so that a weapon hitting them would slide off the armor rather than stick into it. On the Maximilian suits many of the parts have edges with a high ridge or "rope." At first glance these appear to be merely for purposes of decoration; in reality they were made so that when the blade did glance or slide it would catch against the roped edge, to be held there, and so be prevented from slipping between the joints of armor.

When an armorer had toiled away at a suit and at last finished it, in order to insure its powers of protection he was very likely to have it proved. The armor was usually placed upon a mannikin, though occasionally upon a man. If it were mail, it was often given a chopping cut with a heavy sword. The thrust of a poignard, a sharp, slender dagger with a square or triangular-shaped blade, was also a very severe test. If the armor was plate, it was shot at with a heavy crossbow. Having withstood the arrow or bolt, it was then called "proof" armor. If it was tested with the light crossbow or the ordinary war arrow, it was called "half-proof." Certain cities had marks which they put upon their armor showing that it had been proved, such as the lion of St. Mark for the city of Venice or the pine-cone for the city of Augsburg. Occasionally, in addition to this mark, the individual maker added his own proof mark to the suit.

With the coming of Maximilian armor and other elaborate forms, there arose a new group of workers, men who spent all their time in the decoration of armor. They did it in many ways: etching, damascening, gilding, embossing, and what might be termed merely for the sake of convenience, cutting and piercing. This

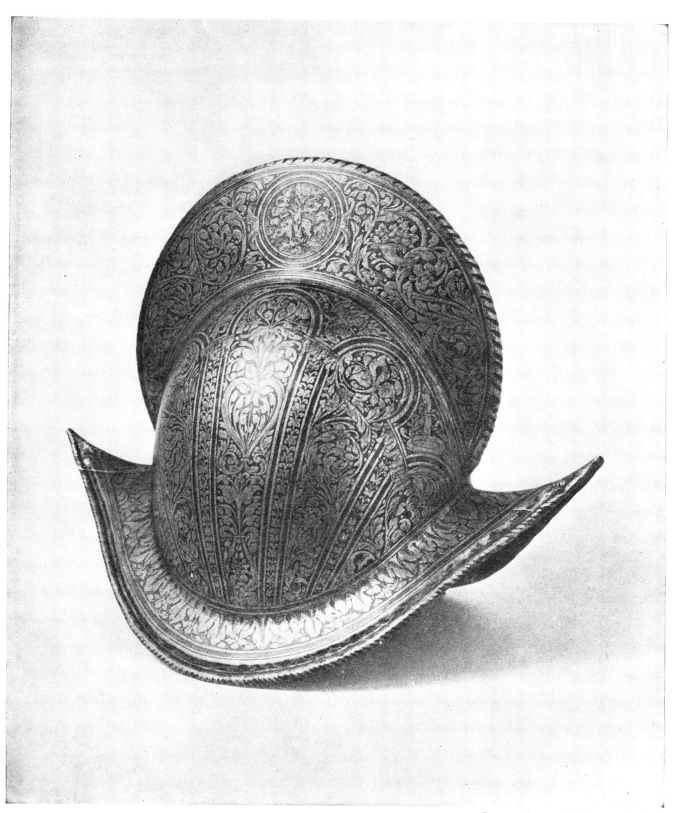

An Etched Decoration on a Helmet.

latter is to be found particularly upon the hand-guards of swords, the later swords. They were wrought until the designs seem like some delicate openwork lace pattern, yet so skillfully were they handled that strength was not sacrificed to any great extent.

Etching was done in two ways, the German and the Italian. With the Italian method, the whole surface was covered with wax or varnish. The design was drawn with a sharp-pointed instrument that scraped away the varnish; the little dots in the background were also laid bare by a touch of the etcher's tool. When the pattern

Courtesy of The Cleveland Museum of Art.

Process of Etching.

was complete, the surface was given an acid bath. The acid ate away the bright metal and left what was covered with varnish standing out in relief. The German method exactly reversed the Italian. In the German method the design was put on with the varnish and the dots made by depositing little globules of it in the background. When this was laid in the bath, the acid ate away the background rather than the design. The best way of telling whether a given piece of armor was etched by the German or by the Italian method is to look at the little dots very carefully. They are more regular in size and shape when done by the German method. The etching upon the Maximilian suit was done in the German way.

Damascening is a process of inlaying a harder metal with a softer, usually iron

Courtesy   Cleveland Museum of Art.

Process of Damascening.

[62]

with gold. It is a painstaking process and had its origin in the East, where time was of less account than in the bustling western world. In damascening, the design is made upon the iron with a sharp tool which leaves a track with burred edges. When the gold is beaten into the track prepared for it, the little nicks help to clamp the gold in place. A second way of damascening is to scratch the surface crisscross so that when the gold is pounded in, it will be clamped firmly in position.

Often parts of a suit were gilded, or occasionally a whole suit. The surface to which the gilt was to be applied was made immaculately clean. The gilt was a mixture of mercury, or quicksilver, and gold, finely pounded. These were heated

Courtesy of The Cleveland Museum of Art.

Process of Gilding.

together in a crucible until they were thoroughly combined or fused; and the resulting amalgam was applied to the iron with a wire brush. When the desired surface was completely covered, it was heated "over a slow fire till all the quicksilver goes off in fumes," says Cellini, "leaving the shining coating pure gilt." Then the whole was burnished to a high polish.

The process of embossing is the art of raising designs upon metal by hammering. After duly preparing his plate, the armorer traced his design on the front, marking its outline with a punch, the indentations of which were clearly visible on the back. He then placed the plate face downward upon a yielding surface, usually pitch.

With hammers and punches he beat the design into relief, working alternately on front and back. His tools included not only these punches and hammers of

[63]

Process of Embossing. A Colletin.

various kinds for tracing, raising, grounding, and texturing the surfaces, but also a special small anvil called a "snarl." This small anvil with a projecting point on one side was common in the fifteen hundreds. The projecting point was introduced into a hollow where a hammer or a punch could not enter easily. It took endless skill to handle the metal during the early stage of the process and infinite patience to put the necessary final finish upon it. None but an artist could have accomplished the task. The raised design on a finely executed colletin, or neck defense, shows what beauty can be wrought by this method of decoration.

But decoration was only a small part of the making of any piece of armor. A full-page illustration* shows the various steps which had to be taken in forging a helmet. It is only necessary to think of the hard and stubborn qualities of a flat piece of iron to get an idea of the difficulties in store for the armorer. The plate in (1) of the illustration is about twenty inches in diameter. The metal is heated from time to time, and by repeated blows of the hammer the plate is spread in such a way that the center begins to rise a little; it takes the form of a saucer turned upside down (2). Next it becomes cone-shaped (4). It then develops the central ridge or comb (5). This comb is of great value to the wearer of the helmet as it protects him where blows rain hardest and forms in addition an excellent glancing surface. Next, the sides are produced (6). After that the work progresses from stage to stage in an orderly

* The description of this illustration is adapted, by slightly simplifying the vocabulary, from "Helmets and Body Armor in Modern Warfare," Bashford Dean, Ph.D.

sequence. Much of the later work was done on unheated metal, which, however, was softened from time to time. The armorer worked on his metal cold, although it was more difficult to do so, because the final result was a harder, stronger helmet. To understand how laborious the steps are, it is only necessary to realize that to make a helmet costs several months' hard and conscientious work. It will be seen that the artist controlled his metal very completely. He could push it into regions where it would be needed, such as the crest or comb of the helmet, where the hardest blows were apt to fall.

As the helmet was built up step by step, so were all the intricate plates of a complete suit of armor. The men who did the best work on such helmets and suits were as well known as the great painters and sculptors of their day. Each man's work was carefully signed with a mark which could not be used by any other man. Some of the most famous armorers were Lorenz Colman (1516), Coloman Colman (1476-1532), and Desiderius Colman (about 1532) of Augsburg; Thomaso Missaglia (about 1415-1468) and his son Antonio Missaglia (1530-1592) of Milan; Philippo and Jacomo Negroli (about 1521-1580), also of Milan; and Conrad, Hans, and Jorg Seusenhofer (1470-1555), each one of whom was at some time armorer to the Emperor Maximilian.

While the great painters of Europe have left a large number of pictures for us to see, only a few suits made by each of the great armorers mentioned have been preserved. Battles, rain, and rust have destroyed the mighty work of their forges. Most of the armor found in our museums was made by unknown craftsmen, like the weavers of tapestry or the brothers of the pen. These armorers hammered their lives out in cold iron. What we know of them is but the burnished surfaces they left behind—a goodly monument.

It is said that the test of a fine workman is his tools—the kind he uses and the condition in which they are kept. If this is the case, the armorer proves him-

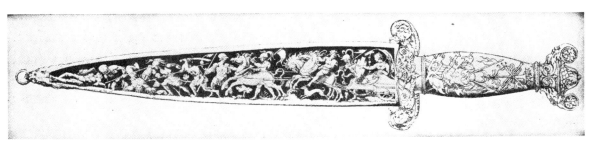

Courtesy of The Metropolitan Museum of Art.

A Design for a Dagger, by Hans Holbein.

[65]

A Helmet with Bands of Gilding.

self to be a master indeed. Some of his old tools have come down to us. They are many of them as carefully decorated as is the armor. An anvil, shown in the illustration of the armorer's shop, has columns and arches beaten into its surface. A vise has the head of a woman upon it, together with a very charming floral design. Guardian over all is the statue of St. Eligius with the leg of the fractious horse in his hand. The shop itself is a marvel of the wood-carver's art; walls and doorway are cut into patterns as delicate as shadows. Compare this with a modern factory. In the little shop with its hand-wrought tools, its carving, its decorated anvil, there still lingers the spirit of the ancient craftsman who demanded

1. PLATE OF MACHINE-TOOL STEEL
(13/100 in.thick) FROM WHICH
HELMET IS MADE

2. PLATE GIVING FIRST CURVATURE,
CHALKLINE DENOTES FUTURE
CREST

3. PLATE DEVELOPED BOWL SHAPED.
NOTE DEEP MARKS OF HAMMER

4. BOWL ASSUMES CONICAL FORM

5. DOME OF HEAD AND CREST
APPEAR

6. SIDES NOW DEVELOPED

7. MARGIN CUT OFF, OUTLINING FACE

8. NECK REGION ARISING

9. CRANIUM MODELLED.
NOTE HAMMER MARKS
INSIDE AND OUT

10. SIDE VIEW OF
SOMEWHAT LATER
STAGE

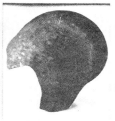

11. SIDES CUT OUT
FOR FITTING
CHEEK-PLATES

12. FRONT VIEW OF
SIMILAR STAGE

13. CREST AND NECK
REGION COMPLETED

14. CHEEK PIECES
IN PLACE

15. VISOR AND VENTAIL
ATTACHED

16. BOWL, CHEEK-PIECES,
VISOR, AND VENTAIL
IN PLACE

17. FILED AND POLISHED,
BORDERS FINISHED, BANDS
READY FOR DECORATION

18. READY FOR ETCHING.
PATTERN PAINTED IN
ACID-PROOF VARNISH

19. DECORATED BANDS
FIRE-GILT.
HELMET FINISHED

20. FRONT VIEW OF
FINISHED HELMET
WEIGHT 8½ POUNDS

21. SIDE VIEW OF
FINISHED HELMET

PHOTOGRAPHS SHOWING HOW A HELMET IS MADE

1-13, BOWL HAMMERED OUT OF A SINGLE PIECE OF STEEL; 14-16, PARTS PUT TOGETHER;
17, FILED AND POLISHED; 18, READY FOR ETCHING; 19-21, FIRE-GILT AND FINISHED.

HELMET NOW IN GALLERY H-8 CASE 95, WORK BY D. TACHAUX, 1915,
IN RESTORING THE MISSING HEAD-PIECE OF SCUDAMORE ARMOR.

A Damascened Medallion from a Shield.

not only that his armor should be excellent, but that the very implements with
which he toiled should be works of art, and that the walls which rose about him
should reflect his hopes and ambitions.

The Armorer's Shop.

Courtesy of The Metropolitan Museum of Art.

This, and the designs on pages 50 and 51, are for scabbard mountings.
All three are designed by Peter Flötner.

In the Great Days of the City of Florence A Foreword

Florence was a city of great artists and craftsmen, all of whom were gallant gentlemen, many of whom were hardy adventurers. From this illustrious group five men have been selected for the next five chapters. A little girl who very kindly wrote her opinion of the Ghiberti chapter before it was published said: "If I were you, I wouldn't have Ghiberti work for forty-eight years on two doors."

When the writer read this, she was horrified. The Ghiberti chapter is not a made-up story; none of the chapters are. They are accounts of what actually happened, written as accurately as the writer knew how. How could Ghiberti be made to spend less than forty-eight years, since forty-eight years *he did spend*? As well ask a historian please to have Columbus discover the route to India, for which he was searching, instead of America. After all, if great artists of the past chose to live in a certain way, there is nothing to be done about it, unless it is to explain very carefully that what is written here—with the exception of the legends, most of them printed in a different type—is fact. In the hands of fact, the writer is helpless, quite.

Ghiberti And The Goblins

GHIBERTI AND THE GOBLINS

In Florence one day in the year 1378 the streets were filled with crowds just as usual. There were messengers of the great families of Florence in wonderful rich colors: reds, blues, greens, and golds; there were market women with luscious fruits, round cabbages, and long purple beans; there were the hardy citizens talking of this or that; there was the sound of chanting as brown-robed monks walked in solemn procession along the streets; a sound of laughing and hooting as a wild and merry troop of boys dashed down some narrow passageway, almost upsetting a fat burgher with a basket on his arm. These boys were out for mischief, nothing less.

The sun shone in the blue sky just as usual. Dark shadows were thrown across the street by towers with square battlements and towers with pointed ones. These towers reminded the city of the days when Florence was torn in twain by two groups of nobles fighting against each other. The towers with square battlements had belonged to the Guelphs, who were loyal to the Church and enemies of the Empire and of the Ghibellines. The towers with the pointed battlements had belonged to the Ghibellines, who were loyal to the Empire and enemies to the Church and so to the Guelphs. Prominent among these towers was the tower of the Bargello, where now the ruler in the name of the Empire was housed, the nobleman from a foreign court known to the people of Florence as the *podestà*. The Bargello cast the blackest shadow of all. But only the very old men and the young, adventurous and discontented, thought of that.

As always, Florence was gay and busy. In the shops of the goldsmiths, little hammers tapped as usual. In the wood-carver's shop the shavings dropped to the floor as usual in a golden rain. In the large rooms of the sculptors, clay was poked and punched unmercifully or marble trembled from the blows of the chisel. In the dyer's house, red, blue, purple, yellow pots of dye gleamed in the sunlight. In the weavers' quarters, the tapestry weavers told strange tales in threads of wool, gold, and silver. All was just as usual, just as if one of her greatest artists was not being born in Florence that day. Within a short time he was taken to the church

The Baptistry, Florence.

of St. John—San Giovanni, his parents called it. There was often a christening going on in San Giovanni, so often that it was sometimes spoken of as the Baptistry. That was what it was for—christenings; hadn't San Giovanni himself baptized the Lord Jesus in the River Jordan, and wasn't he the patron saint of Florence? No one paid much attention to the little swaddled bunch in his mother's arms, but the day was to come when the Baptistry was to know Lorenzo Ghiberti well.

He grew up as did any other Italian *bambino*. He learned to walk in the sunny open court of his house; and almost before any one knew it, he was out on the streets playing and yelling with the other boys, dashing down some narrow passageway and almost knocking over a pompous steward with a flagon of wine in his hand. Soon this, too, came to an end. Lorenzo's stepfather, the good Bartolo di Michele, led the boy to his *bottega,* his shop, one morning, that the lad might become an apprentice there and learn the goldsmith's craft.

Lorenzo took to the work like a duck to water. Soon he was able to twist the wires of a filigree brooch or chain until they made patterns as delicate as frost. He was wise in choosing the settings for his jewels, clever in hammering and cutting the long pear-shaped earrings that were worn by the grand ladies of his day. He spent long hours over his designs, drawing and planning.

But Ghiberti was not satisfied with this, although he could soon do his work as well as Bartolo himself. The boy wandered through the streets of Florence looking for a new idea in the shadows of an old wall, or on the richly embroidered cope of the priests as they walked in some procession. While he wandered, Ghiberti looked more and more often at the statues made by great sculptors of Florence; he stood long in front of the high tower of the cathedral; above all, he marveled at the doors of the Baptistry, made by the wonderful artist, Andrea Pisano.

He was not satisfied. Beside such things as these, his delicate earrings, his carefully wrought bracelets and chains seemed only toys. He wanted to become a sculptor. Often his workbench was empty, and the patient Bartolo would find him grubby with clay or sticky with wax, modeling some figure: a dog, perhaps, a pig, a donkey, and after a while a man, woman, or even an angel. So well did he do his tasks that Bartolo complained little when his own orders were late. He knew an artist when he saw one; he knew that the young apprentice needed time and room in which to work out his thoughts. He even helped the boy cast his figures in bronze, find models, mix his colors, and prepare his wooden panel when he turned, as he often did, from sculpture to painting.

[76]

While the young artist was still working, a little for Bartolo and a great deal for himself, a terrible plague broke out in Florence. In company with a friend, a painter, he fled to Romagna, some miles from the stricken city. There, together with his companion, he painted a chamber for Signor Pandolfo Malatesti, greatly to that gentleman's satisfaction. Yet all the while Lorenzo was at work with his wax, stucco, and other materials, practicing as sculptors must.

When the plague died down, he received a message from Bartolo, a very important message. The Signoria, that is to say, the governors of Florence, and the Guild of Merchants had decided, after much talking and learned deliberation, that the time had come for the church of San Giovanni to have new doors. The doors were to be made in such a way as to be worthy companions to those of Andrea Pisano, the doors at which Lorenzo had marveled when but a lad. The magistrates and the Guild of Merchants had sent word out all over Italy that artists would be welcome in Florence. Each was to make a sculptured panel, and the artist whose work was most successful was to be selected as the master to create the new doors. It was this message which the young Ghiberti received from his stepfather.

An Old Historian tells how Bartolo wrote to the young man: "And if by the Grace of Our Lady you should win this work, then you will no longer be vexed by baubles and pear-making." By "pear-making" of course Bartolo meant the pear-shaped earrings that all the fine ladies were asking the goldsmiths for, and over which the goldsmiths toiled, hour after hour. Though all the courts of Romagna were entreating him to remain, and though he had won much fame, fair fortune, and good friends, Lorenzo was soon on the road to Florence. Every moment seemed an hour until he saw its towers grim against the blue, blue sky.

A great many artists had already arrived before him. Together with them, he presented himself before the consuls of the guilds, who chose seven masters from the whole number; three of these were Florentines, among them Lorenzo. The remaining four came from other towns in Tuscany. Each artist was given a sum of money and commanded to tell a story in bronze according to his skill.

The sculptors, who cast their own work in bronze as did all the craftsmen of Ghiberti's day, had before them a delicate and difficult task, which it is well to know a little about in order to understand their work better. Bronze is a metal made of a combination of copper and tin. It was used by the ancients as a means of making their statues permanent because it is a very lasting as well as a very beautiful material. Just as it was used long ago, it is still used to-day.

Photograph by Alinari.

Panel from the Doors at the Main Entrance of the Baptistry,
by Lorenzo Ghiberti.
The Story of Jacob and Esau.

The panels for the Baptistry doors were in all probability made by what is known as the "lost wax" process. The panel was first of all modeled in clay somewhat roughly. Then over the clay was put a layer of wax just the thickness that the bronze was desired to be. The wax was modeled very carefully, for from it the finished work would take its shape. Over the wax was put a mold or matrix, that is, the wax was covered by a paste made of pounded brick, ashes, and clay mixed with water until it was about the thickness of cream. This was combined very carefully and pressed even more carefully into all the little curves of the wax. When it had dried, it fitted closely like a hard outer skin.

As even greater protection for the precious work within, more clay was packed on the outside until the panel looked like a shapeless mass, rather like a cocoon with the precious butterfly inside. The whole was bound with bands of iron to keep each part in place. Then the panel was put in a furnace, where the mold of brick, clay, and ashes was baked until it was entirely hard. Of course the wax melted away leaving a hollow space where it had been. Into this hollow, bronze, heated until it had become liquid, was poured.

Long hours, days passed before the outer shell could be broken away. Then only, could the sculptor know whether or not his work had been made lasting and beautiful by the bronze or utterly ruined by some jar, some sudden change in temperature, a mistake in mixing the materials for the mold. A hundred things might happen and the labor of months then be as nothing. The casting was a time of great anxiety and excitement for the sculptor. If all went well, he saw before him in bronze what his skillful hands had modeled from wax; he saw a statue or a panel that would last long years after his fingers had lost their cunning.

This casting in bronze, difficult as it was, played a small part in any sculptor's task. He had first of all to think how he was to tell his story, what figures he would put upon his panel, where he would place them. He must have people enough to tell his tale, yet not too many to crowd his space; the lines of his figures must move well within the lines of his background. The whole must make a design or pattern. When once these difficulties became clear to him, the good Lorenzo's hands must follow quickly and well the command of his brain. There was no time to wonder how to do this, what tool to use here, when to finish this curve, when to begin that. These questions were answered by the years of practice he had put upon his craft, and by the looking and wondering he had done while still a little boy. Now he was at work in clay and wax. He could no longer think how; he must know and do.

With idea after idea whirling through his quick brain, the young sculptor started eagerly upon his task. The subject for all the panels made by different artists was to be the same. It was the Bible story of how Abraham, thinking that he had received a command from his God, took his son, Isaac, up on the mountain to offer him as a sacrifice upon an altar there. Just as, weeping and sorrowful, Abraham was about to slay his son in answer to the command of Jehovah, an angel appeared saying that mercy was granted both to him and to the frightened child, Isaac. Both were saved from the grim deed.

Bartolo di Michele worked with Ghiberti, encouraging and helping. The Old Historian says that Bartolo "suffered him to shrink from no amount of labor," and saw to it that he made many trials before he decided on any one plan. None of the other artists would allow any stranger to see their work, but Lorenzo opened his doors wide and listened well to all that was said.

"That figure is too stiff," frowned a bent old shoemaker who sat at his awl hour after hour and watched the good Florentines pass him; he knew a thing or two. "The angel is too heavy; it does not float," said a boy of nine. He watched birds; he knew what it was like to fly. He had a pet dove of his own at home. "Those mountains do not tower high enough," sighed a tanned stranger who had just made a perilous journey over the Alps. "They tower too high," growled a farmer who had never in all his life lifted his eyes from his flat fields. "It is foolish to put an ass in your panel," simpered a haughty and delicate lady. "How else would Abraham and Isaac have got up the mountain?" laughed a wine vendor who came from the hills of Fiesole and went back every day on his good gray donkey. Out of all the words of the wise and the foolish, Lorenzo chose those which would help him on his difficult way; and at last he made a model which the Old Historian says "was without any defect whatever."

Ghiberti then took his last step; and through hours of toil, of watching, of waiting, of lighting a candle to the Virgin in prayer, of sitting up nights, of laboring until dawn, of tears, of anger, of fear, hours of joy and hope, despair and endless weariness, the panel was at last cast in bronze. Lorenzo Ghiberti with Bartolo's help polished the whole "with such love and care and patience that no work could be executed with more care or finished with greater delicacy."

The day came at last for judging. Thirty-four artists from without the city as well as many within were called to give their opinions. There were two panels wondrously well wrought, one by Brunelleschi, the master builder of Florence, the other by Lorenzo Ghiberti. Of the panel done by Lorenzo, the judges said that "all was finished with so much care as to perfection, that the work seemed not to have been cast and polished with instruments of iron, but looked rather as though it had been blown with breath." So it was that Lorenzo Ghiberti won the competition when but a youth of twenty.

For twenty-one years this man was at work upon the doors, planning, modeling, casting each of the twenty-eight panels separately. Each of the panels told one

The Doors at the Main Entrance of the Baptistry, by Lorenzo Ghiberti.

chapter in the life of Jesus. Together they tell the whole story with very great beauty and understanding. As a molding for the door frame, inclosing the whole, he made garlands that seem to grow, with heads of young angels, the lithe bodies of little squirrels, birds, and children peeping through the foliage.

When the great task was finished, a feast was held. All the fathers of the church in their scarlet robes, the ruler of Florence and his train, the great council of the Signoria, the butcher, the baker, the candlestick-maker; rich man, poor man, beggar man, thief, doctor, lawyer, merchant, chief; the fuller and the armorer, the furrier and the dyer, scamps and cheats, monks and nuns, fine ladies and rich old women and young children—children everywhere: on their fathers' shoulders, on the tops of buildings, on their tiptoes, almost falling out of windows, waving from balconies, children all eyes for one Lorenzo Ghiberti filled the streets of Florence on that day when the doors were hung in the church of San Giovanni, where he, himself, had been christened some forty years before.

After the doors were in place, the fame of Lorenzo spread all over Italy; and orders came to him from churches and castles, from Pope and Cardinal. The city of Florence, having gained great honor from his work, decided to move the old doors made by Andrea Pisano and have new doors made for the main entrance of the Baptistry by Lorenzo. This time the subject was to be stories from the Old Testament. For twenty-seven years Ghiberti labored, building up his work, panel by panel. Forty-eight years went into the making of two pairs of doors. When Ghiberti began them, he was a light-hearted youth; when he finished them, he was an old man, weary and bent with toil. Yet despite his weariness he finished his days happy and honored, living quietly in his beloved city. He had made the most wonderful doors ever looked upon. With every day that passed over him, he had added to the world a beauty that had not been there before. He captured it and held it fast in the bronze of his panels.

This is the story of the bronze doors as history tells it to us, but history does not know everything. When the people—not the wise and learned, the scholars and priests, but the common folk such as the peasant Antonio or his wife Maria, her boy Beppo or the flower girl Santina—when these looked at the doors, they said to one another, "Surely no man, no matter how clever his hand or how wise his head, no man could have made these doors alone. There is the spirit of the Bargello who wears a red cap; there are the *fatae* (fairies) good and bad. My son Niccolo saw a wee tiny lamp shining just beyond the sail of his boat last week, and it led him all astray."

A Detail of Molding from the Main Doors of the Baptistry,
by Lorenzo Ghiberti.

"And my Lucia had a wee thing jump into the milk pail; and though she had just finished her milking, the milk had turned as sour as a scolding old dame." So they marveled, the folk that looked; and as they looked they marveled more; and all the while they talked to themselves and to one another. Thus there grew up among the folk the story of "Ghiberti and the Goblins," which would surely

Photograph by Alinari.

A Trial Panel, by Lorenzo Ghiberti.

[84]

have made the good Lorenzo laugh if he had happened to hear it, he who had worked for forty-eight years on two doors. Yet still the folk said: "Surely no man could have made these gates alone." And they told the tale like this:

When Ghiberti was at work upon the very first panel, hoping to be chosen to make the new doors, he suddenly found himself bewitched. A sorceress, Chanetta, had a grievous spite against him; and she cast a spell over him. Whatever he tried to do turned out just the opposite. If he tried to model an angel, he saw before him a demon; and when he was at work on an ass, it turned into a dragon. So great was the grief of Lorenzo that he threw his tools aside and could toil no more; neither could he hope for relief. At last another witch, Teodora, who had heard of his trouble with the evil Chanetta, came to his aid, saying, "O Lorenzo, why do you moan and sit disconsolate day by day? Why do you cry out in sleep and rise weary with the dawn?"

Then did Lorenzo tell her how a spell had been cast over him so that his hand had lost its cunning and his brain, its wisdom.

"Good Lorenzo," said Teodora, "this is indeed a grievous tale. The witch Chanetta has great power, as great as mine, so that I cannot break the spell, but I will call the Goblins. For you must know the world is full of Goblins. The Goblins are often sad; they live for only a thousand years; they are not immortal like the fairies. And worse than that, they fear much, for when they die they may have to become devils. There is but one way in which they can be saved. If the Goblins can dwell within the carved figures of saints or angels, whether on the altar or on the column or door of a church, they will live always and never have to become demons. I will call the Goblins."

That night as the clock struck twelve, the witch Teodora entered the great hall where Ghiberti had been at work vainly trying to cast his panel in bronze. She called the Goblins; in witchy whispers she called them:

All wingèd Goblins, come ye here!
If ye wish to be like fairies
All unfettered by the years
Come ye here!
Ye shall fly both swift and free
Under heavens blue and gold.
Come ye here,
And be turned to little figures

Made of shining bronze,
Figures in the mighty doorway
Of the church of San Giovanni.
Come ye here!
Be an ass, an angel, fruit,
Be a squirrel, a leaf, a flower;
Be a dove, a king, a saint;
Be a lamb, a priest, a tree.

All wingèd Goblins, come ye here!
Come ye here!

From east, from west, from north, from south, from over the moon and under the sun, riding on the drops of dew, coasting down the starlight, sliding on a planet's beams, holding to the whiskers that shadows have, on came the Goblins. The Goblins came in dozens and tens, in hundreds and twos, in fives and nines, in sevens and threes. Their wee feet tapped like scuttering mice, their bat wings flapped like fairy sails; their round eyes gleamed like jewels that wink. On came the Goblins. Teodora told the Goblins of her plan; with moon-lit words she told it, and the Goblins hung in silent circles to hear her words.

When morning came, Ghiberti returned despairing to his task. And it was finished, though he had not lifted his hand! The Goblins had taken the form of the little figures on the bronze panel. So well had they done their work that when the judges looked upon the panel, they said, "Lorenzo shall make the doors." Nor was that the last time the Goblins helped him. Years later when the last panel was put in place and the doors hung at the main entrance of the Baptistry, so beautifully had the Goblins posed that the great sculptor Michelangelo said, "These doors are worthy to be the gates of Paradise."

The folk told how long ago there were many and now there still be a few who, if they stand in front of the church of San Giovanni on a moonless night, can see the little bat-winged figures flit in and out of their bronze dwelling-place. For the Goblins have become immortal as has the beauty of Ghiberti's doors.

Photograph by Alinari.

Panels from the North Door of the Baptistry, by Lorenzo Ghiberti.
Christ Driving the Money Changers from the Temple.
Christ with His Disciples on the Sea of Galilee.

That is what the peasant Antonio or his wife Maria, her boy Beppo or the flower girl Santina said. How the good Lorenzo would have smiled had he known, he who worked for forty-eight years on two doors. And yet . . . strange things happen on a moonless night. Who knows!

[86]

The North Doors of the Baptistry, Florence, by Lorenzo Ghiberti.

Capping the Duomo — Brunelleschi

CAPPING THE DUOMO

Five hundred and fifty years ago a lad named Filippo Brunelleschi was growing up in Florence just as Lorenzo Ghiberti or any other small Italian boy grew up, save that Filippo was given more learning than most. His father, Ser Brunelleschi, a notary, early began to teach him his letters; and great was the good man's distress when he found that his son had little liking for books. Filippo was always making things with his hands, building with stones and blocks of wood while he was but a baby, and later working out many very ingenious mechanical devices. Not a little troubled, Ser Brunelleschi gave up the hope of making a notary of his son and saw to it that, though Filippo had a chance to learn writing and arithmetic, the boy spent most of his time in a shop where he became acquainted with the goldsmith's difficult craft.

While the young Lorenzo Ghiberti worked with his stepfather, a goldsmith, Filippo likewise hammered all day at the same trade. He was glad enough to be done with thick books and long words. He handled the little hammers with such skill that soon there was nothing about the trade he did not know, whether it were the setting of jewels, the making of a bit of enamel, or the carving of a gem. He also made two figures in silver for a church altar that were considered very beautiful both by the priests and by the folk.

All this time he was also working at his mechanics; he thought very hard about the adjustments of weights, the movement of wheels, all that has to do with the making of clocks, adding much to man's knowledge of them. Not content with that, Filippo turned his attention to sculpture. At this time he fell in with a young lad called Donatello, who likewise cared a great deal for carving and modeling, so much so, indeed, that he gave all his time to it. Filippo, on the other hand, not only continued his work as a mechanic, goldsmith, and sculptor, but also took to decorating and rebuilding houses.

The Old Historian tells how in those days Donatello completed a crucifix in wood and desired to have the opinion of his friend in regard to the work; but he was sorry indeed that he had asked, since Filippo replied that Donatello had

The Pantheon, Rome.

Photograph by Alinari.

placed "a clown on the cross." "Take wood then and make one for yourself," said the young Donatello, not a little angered. Therefore, Filippo, who never allowed himself to be irritated by his companion, kept silence for several months while preparing a crucifix, also in wood, of a size similar to Donatello's. When it was finished, he summoned his friend. Donatello stopped on the way to Filippo's to do a bit of marketing and entered the room with his apron full of purchases. When he saw the crucifix, he so marveled at its excellence that he dropped the corners of his apron. Eggs smashed, cheeses split their bags, cabbages ran chasing one another, and a fowl lay on its back helpless, with both feet sticking straight up.

Brunelleschi's crucifix, which almost ruined dinner for the two of them, is to be seen to-day over an altar in what is known as the Gondi Chapel in the Church of Santa Maria Novella. In this same year Lorenzo Ghiberti won for himself the wonderful task of making new doors for the Baptistry. Brunelleschi lost it, though every one said his work had been done wondrously well. Great was his disappointment; by way of consoling himself he left Florence with Donatello and traveled to the city of Rome. By this time, the Old Historian says, Filippo and Donatello were "so strongly attached that the one seemed unable to live without the other."

Happily enough, the two of them traveled along the busy highways to the city of the Pope. Once arrived, Filippo, deciding that the art of building—architecture—was more useful to man than either painting or sculpture, turned his thought to this. He measured all the old buildings in Rome, drew plans of them, copied their columns and their arches until he could see with his mind's eye how the whole city must have looked when the great Caesar Augustus drove his chariot through its marble-lined streets.

The artists were so constantly to be seen working over old walls and foundations, prying here, digging there, that they became known in the city as the "treasure-seekers"; and this name they frequently heard as they passed along in their dusty tunics. The reason for this name was the fact that once the two had dug up an old earthenware vase filled with ancient coins. But they were seeking no money treasure; they were trying to find anew some of the wonderful secrets known to the ancients—secrets about the way they built their buildings, secrets about the carving of stones, the decorations of their temples and courts.

One building in particular Filippo studied and drew until he knew it inside and out, up and down. It was the great Pantheon with its marvelous dome, the largest dome anywhere in all Europe. Filippo was thinking more about that than

The Pitti Palace, Florence.

(The original design was made by Brunelleschi, but the palace has been greatly enlarged since then.)

about anything else, because in the city of Florence the great cathedral—Duomo—was then without a dome. The cathedral had never been finished because no one knew how to build a dome for it. Roofed over as it was in Brunelleschi's day, it looked flat and almost bowed down as if it mourned the fact that its chief glory was lacking. So diligently did Filippo work at the Pantheon that there was hardly an inch of the heavy concrete walls and dome which he did not know as well as the palm of his own hand.

That he had done this work was well, for while he was still in Rome an assemblage of architects was called together in Florence by the superintendent of the works of the cathedral and by the syndics of the Guild of Wool-Workers to consult as to how the cupola for the cathedral should be made, how the Duomo should be capped. Among the other artists appeared Filippo, for when he heard the news he

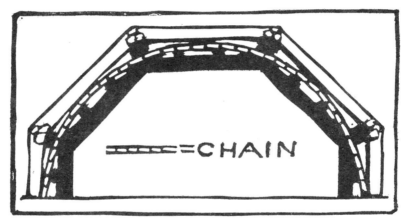

The Chain Which Kept the Dome from Spreading.

hastened to Florence with all speed. He told the magistrates and the syndics of his plan; but they deliberated so long that Filippo returned again to Rome, thinking that he might enjoy more reputation if he were at a distance. So difficult was the problem that the more the magistrates and syndics deliberated the more mixed up they became, and at last they summoned Filippo again to Florence along with a large number of foreign masters.

A fine thing it was to hear all the ideas that were proposed. One worthy thought to heap up a pile of earth in which coins had been scattered, build the dome over it, then call the peasants and the poor folk, who would scramble for the coins and so cart off the earth. Filippi alone declared that the cupola might be raised without a great mass of woodwork, without a column in the center, and without the mound of earth. Hearing this, the syndics, who were expecting a very complicated plan from Filippo,

Brunelleschi's Dome, a Landmark for all Florence.

Photograph by Alinari.

decided that he was nothing more nor less than a simpleton. They laughed at him for a mad man; and as he walked the streets, the people hooted at him; and the small boys danced about him, teasing and making fun. But Filippo said to the syndics: "Consider, gentlemen, that it is not possible to raise the cupola in any other way than mine; and although you laugh at me, yet you will be obliged to admit that it neither must nor can be done in any other manner."

Now the walls of the Duomo were in the form of an octagon, an eight-sided figure. Filippo's problem was to put a great swelling dome upon these walls: no small problem it was. As any one knows who may have tried to build a dome with children's blocks, the work goes very smoothly only about so far; and then the weight of the curve pushes the lower row of blocks out of place and the whole collapses. Filippo knew that he could keep this from happening to his dome by putting a great wooden

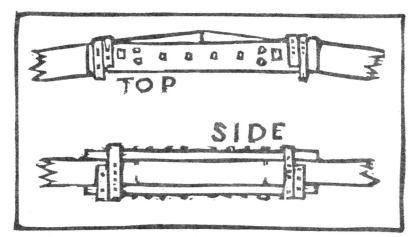

How the Chain Which Bound the Dome of the Cathedral Was Made.

chain about it to hold the lower part in place. When he had fastened the chain securely and passed that danger point in the building, if the work were done carefully no disaster could happen. His circle, growing smaller as he built, could not, of course, fall in upon itself. The ribs of his dome were to be eight great arches. Over this inner dome, seen from the inside of the cathedral, Filippo planned a higher, outer dome, which would be a landmark for all Florence and for the countryside. The thing about his plan that amazed the syndics and magistrates most of all was that he told them he needed no wooden bracing, only light scaffolding for the workmen to stand on, while the dome was being constructed.

When the magistrates and syndics had heard Filippo, they quickly dismissed him and again deliberated among themselves, coming in the end no further than the place

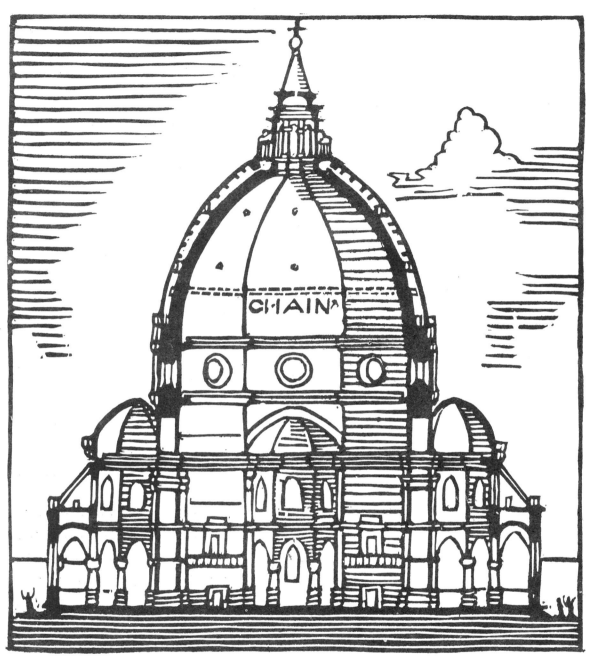

CHAIN

Cross-section of the Dome of the Cathedral, Florence.

This is a drawing of the Cathedral of Florence as if it were sliced in half as you might slice an apple. Just as cutting the apple through the center shows you how the apple grew, the mark of the blossom, the seeds, the stem, so this shows how the cathedral was built: the outer and inner dome, the great lantern, the heavy walls that are the foundation for the dome.

from which they had started in their arguments. Again they assembled the artists from far and near; and at this time, according to the Old Historian, arose the dispute about the egg. The other artists proposed that Filippo should make a model showing just how he would do his work; this Filippo refused to do. "But," said he, "let the one of us who is able to make an egg stand upright on a piece of smooth marble be appointed to build the dome."

Whereupon Filippo, being told that he might make it stand himself, took it daintily into his hand, gave it a blow on the plane of the marble and made it stand upright. Beholding this, the artists protested loudly, saying that they all could easily have done the same; but Filippo replied laughing that they might also know how to construct the dome if they had seen his model.

After only a little more troublesome deliberation the syndics finally gave the building of the dome to Filippo, but they made Lorenzo Ghiberti a fellow-worker with him. This did not please Filippo overmuch, for while Lorenzo Ghiberti knew much of sculpture and casting in bronze, he knew little of building. Had it not been for the encouragement of his friend Donatello and one Luca della Robbia, Filippo would surely have given over his beloved task even before he started it. The Old Historian writes, "The work was . . . continued with but little pleasure on the part of Filippo, who knew that he must endure all the labors connected therewith, and would then have to divide the honor and fame equally with Lorenzo." None the less the work was begun; and Filippo was busy in a thousand ways, with scaffoldings for the masons, with models, with making and fixing the chains. Lorenzo seemed unable to be of any great help to Brunelleschi.

Finally one morning Filippo did not show himself at the works at all. "He tied up his head with great haste and anxiety, pretending that he had an attack of pleurisy." The builders, hearing this, demanded orders of Lorenzo for what they were to do; but he replied that the arrangement of the work belonged to Filippo, and they must wait for him. The illness of Filippo had already lasted more than two days, and the head builders went to see him and repeatedly asked him to tell them what they should do; but he constantly replied, "You have Lorenzo; let him begin to do something for once." Nor could they get anything more from him.

They then went again to Lorenzo, who said to them, "This matter is in the hands of Filippo." And so things went from bad to worse. The whole town was burning with talk, some taking Filippo's side, some Lorenzo's. The wardens, perceiving what discredit came to them from this state of things, went to Filippo and told

The Foundling Hospital, Florence, by Brunelleschi.

him what disorder had come upon the building with his illness; both the stone masons and cutters would work no more. "What," said Filippo, speaking with much heat, "what, is not Lorenzo there? Why does he not do something?" They replied, "He will not do anything without you." He, "But I could do well enough without him."

So it was. By his pretended sickness Filippo proved to all that he and he alone could build the dome of the cathedral. Filippo was made superintendent and chief; nothing was to be done unless he commanded it. Lorenzo, however, was given his salary, which greatly comforted him.

From this time on the work went forward with great ease and rapidity. Filippo was here, there, and everywhere, inventing new ways of lifting heavy stones, and even building, high up in the dome, wine shops and eating houses for the workmen in order that they should not have to endure the fatigue and loss of time that climbing up and down continually would have caused. While the stones for the Duomo were in the hands of the stone-cutters, he would look narrowly to see that they were hard and free from clefts; he supplied the cutters with wax models or hastily made models sliced from turnips to direct them in shaping and judging the various masses. He did the same for the men who prepared the iron work. All the while his good friend Donatello stood ready to help him with words of praise and encouragement.

At last the two vaults of the Duomo were approaching their close. At the top a great lantern was to be placed. Lantern used in this sense, the architectural sense, is not at all a means of producing illumination, but a small tower or cupola through which natural light is admitted. Filippo's lantern was the crown of his dome; he drew complete plans for it, since he was now at an age which made it impossible that he should live to see the whole entirely finished. While he thus labored upon the cathedral, he was called upon by princes and kings to build this, build that, until his name was on every one's lips as that of the greatest architect of his time. Many are the stones which stand to-day in the form which he planned for them, helping to make Florence and indeed numberless other cities the glory which they have become.

On St. Romolo's day, the sixth of July, 1439, seven years before the builder's death, a mighty group of learned men, students, professors, bishops, the Emperor, the Pope (come to hold a great Council in Florence) gathered in the Duomo. Florence was used to processions of wondrous richness, but nothing like this splendor had ever glittered before its half-blinded eyes. Jewels, gold, silver, silk, satin, were as common that day as beggars' rags. As the great Council knelt before the Pope, a "storm of bells" broke forth, pealing to all the winds the greatness of the Church, of Florence, and of Brunelleschi, who, struggling and alone, had capped the great Duomo.

The Cap of the Duomo, by Brunelleschi.

The Pazzi Chapel, Santa Croce, Florence, by Brunelleschi.

Donatello's "Children"

DONATELLO'S "CHILDREN"

Much of Donatello's life was spent under the protection of the great Cosimo de Medici, master over Florence. Cosimo was master of Florence not because he had been elected to rule, as kings and counts sometimes are, but because he was the greatest man of his time and Florence was wise enough to know it and to let herself be guided by him. Cosimo had control of great wealth, both his own and that of the city. This he caused to be spent for large public buildings, for gathering together a great library, for the welfare of private citizens, for carrying on the wars of Florence, and, above all, for the help and encouragement of Florentine artists.

The city palace of the Medici and their country estates were always open to the most famous writers, painters, builders, and sculptors of Florence, and indeed of all Italy. Great banquets were held, where the guests were not counted, where delicate foods were served on silver plates and wines from crystal goblets. Nobles in rich velvets, lovely women in brocaded silks attended these feasts; and nowhere, unless it were in Rome itself, was there such magnificence.

Into the great hall, lighted with hundreds of candles in golden candelabras, gleaming with satins, with jewels, with shining linen, sweet with perfume and incense and rare fruits, would come a dun, gray figure. It was Donatello, the sculptor, dusty and roughly clad, just as he had come from his workroom. The great Cosimo would hail him with a laugh, beckon him to a seat of honor. Soon he would be a center of jokes, of gay talk. All listened to his wise and clever tongue, and all forgot his clay-streaked garments.

One day, however, Cosimo sent Donatello a new suit and a cap of rose-colored velvet. A fine figure of a man, indeed, he was, as he came to the feast next day. All hailed him, and he was fairly deafened by compliments from the ladies. And yet, in a week or so, having worn his finery but twice, he returned it to Cosimo, saying, "It is much too dainty for an old marble-grubber like Donatello!" The truth of the matter probably was that he felt much more comfortable in his old woolens and knew that his generous patron would welcome him no matter how unsuitably clad. Free and at ease, Donatello wandered in and out of the great house

Madonna with Four Cherubim, by Donatello.

of the Medici; and again he would be gone for months, always sure of a hearty greeting when he returned.

The boy, Donato, called by his friends Donatello, was born in the city of Florence in the year 1386, when his future companion, Filippo Brunelleschi, was a lad of nine years, already busy with his building of toy houses. Donatello's father, a wool-carder by trade, was banished from the city during a revolt of citizens known as the Ciompi Riots. Tradition tells us that Donatello was brought up in the family called the Martelli, though this is by no means sure. But certainly the members of the Martelli household were among Donatello's closest friends when he grew older. Donatello, like Filippo Brunelleschi, like Ghiberti, and like Luca della Robbia, was apprenticed to a goldsmith and learned the niceties of this trade. He also studied painting with one Lorenzo di Bicci and entered the academy of St. Luke when he was twenty-six years old to further study this art. But his real interest was in sculpture. The craft of the goldsmith and the art of the painter were for him but a preparation for this art which was to follow.

From his early youth Donatello was the intimate friend of the builder, Brunelleschi. Together they journeyed on foot to Rome, where Brunelleschi studied all the great monuments, and Donatello drew, modeled, looked at any of the ancient statues he could find. So continuously did Donatello labor that when he returned to Florence, he had already won fame as a sculptor. And he was kept busy enough with orders from here and there.

One of the first things he did on his arrival in Florence was to make three statues for three of the great niches in the Church of Or San Michele. Each niche was to be filled with the image of the patron saint of one of the guilds. The guilds of Florence were very powerful and indeed had much to do with governing the city. They were associations of artisans and craftsmen which protected the workers, regulated their wages, decided on the length of their apprenticeship, made sure that the work turned out by each man was good enough to uphold the standard of the craft. In the niches of Or San Michele, among many others, were Donatello's statue of St. Peter, for the Guild of Butchers; St. Mark, probably done by Donatello for the Guild of Flax-Weavers; and Donatello's wonderful St. George, for the Armorers' Guild.

This last figure was remarkable in many ways. It was among the first of the important statues made since the time of the Greeks and Romans which were free-standing. The St. George was not a part of the niche. It could have been placed anywhere, in an open square, for instance, and would have been beautiful looked at from any direction. Before the time of Donatello the figures made by Italian

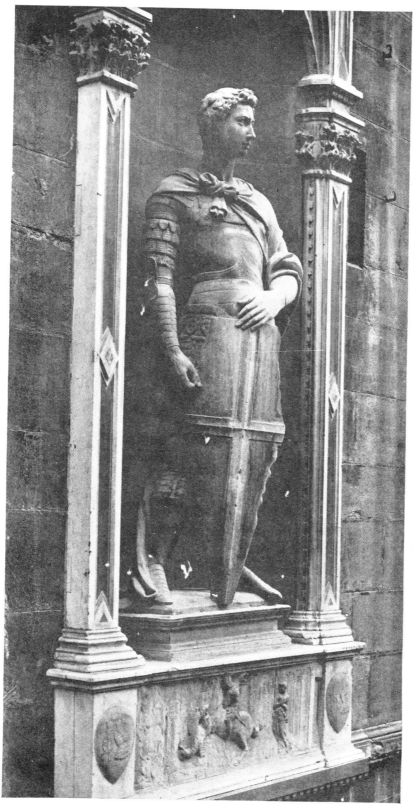

Saint George, by Donatello, Florence.

artists were most of them in what is known as *relief;* that is, they were figures standing out as raised patterns on a flat background, like Donatello's "Children of the Cantoria."

Besides being a step forward, the St. George is in itself one of the most beautiful statues of its day, indeed of any time. It shows the young saint in full armor, his sword girt at his side, his long triangular shield in his hand. He looks fearlessly upon the world, his head held high. At about the same period that Donatello executed the St. George, he also made the figure often called the "Job," so bald a personage that the statue was given the name "il Zuccone," the pumpkin head. This was, of all things he had ever done, Donatello's favorite. As he worked upon it, he would stand off with his chisel in his hand, saying, "Speak then! Plague take thee, why wilt thou not speak?" And when he wanted to say things in such a manner that there could be no doubt, he would say, "By the faith that I place in my Zuccone!"

As he went along the streets in his leathern apron and his clumsy shoes, this great sculptor was hailed on all sides by the most elegant nobles, the raggedest street gamins. He lived like any common workman, and his friends were many of them simple working people. Good comrade as he was, however, Donatello was also a very independent spirit. He was once commissioned to make a portrait bust of a certain Genoese merchant. When it was finished and the time come for payment, the merchant complained that the price was too high.

The matter was finally referred to the great Cosimo de Medici, who caused the bust to be carried to the upper court of the palace and placed between the battlements overlooking the street so that he might see it better. Cosimo then suggested that the price was too small; but the merchant replied that the bust had taken the sculptor less than a month to do, and at that rate the sum he must pay would amount to more than a half florin a day. Whereupon Donatello turned about in great anger; and, telling the merchant that he found means in the hundredth part of an hour to spoil the whole labor and care of a year, he gave a mighty blow to the bust.

Down on the street below, people dodged this way and that; children howled with joy at the excitement; a haughty lady was infuriated because the horse she was riding became terrified and began to run away. Dogs barked, cats scurried this way and that, and it is said that a man who had stolen a pig that day thought justice was after him and ran all the way to Padua without stopping. All this because Donatello had sent his bust crashing over the battlements, at the same time observing to the merchant that he was better at bargaining for horse-beans than

Angel Musicians, Padua, by Donatello.

at purchasing statues. Regretting what had happened, the merchant would have been willing to pay double the price; but Donatello would in no way hear of reconstructing the bust, even upon the request of his good friend and patron, Cosimo de Medici.

In the year 1443 Donatello was invited to Padua, where he decorated the high altar of the Church of San Antonio and also made his wonderful statue of the General Gattamelata seated upon his spirited horse. This was the first large bronze of a horse rider that had been cast in Italy since the days of the ancients, and it is among the most wonderful ever cast. So greatly did the Paduans honor Donatello for his great statue and for the high altar that they besought him to remain among them as their fellow-citizen. But Donatello was determined to return to Florence. "If I stayed here any longer," he said, "I should forget all I have ever known through being so much praised. Willingly, therefore, I return home where I get censured continually; such censure gives occasion for study and brings as a consequence greater glory." Accordingly, he set out on his journey, stopping only in Venice to carve a statue for the Church of the Frari there.

It is little wonder that Donatello wanted to return home, for his home was among the most delightful places in all Florence. Donatello was more than generous with his worldly goods, "being," the Old Historian says, "ever more careful for his friends than for himself." He thought little of his gains but kept what money he had in a basket suspended by a cord from the roof, and from this his assistants as well as his friends took what they needed without being expected to say anything about it. His house was half a dwelling-place, half a workshop— a *bottega*. His assistants were frequently with him, sitting at his long table. A gay lass waited upon them, bringing fine goats'-milk cheeses, roast fowl, and good red wine. Children sat at the table, too, children of his good friends, the Martelli family, who had befriended him in his youth, children rosy-cheeked, full of mischief, with their noses buried in their bowls of soup but their eyes taking in everything.

Bright scarfs and tunics, red, blue, yellow, twinkled amid the earthenware dishes and piles of crisp bread, fruits, and green lentils. The talk ran high: of Ghiberti's doors for the Church of San Giovanni, of Donatello's statue of San Giovanni himself, of the horse race to be held in the great square on the morrow. Often the children demanded a story, and some one would tell of the Red Imp of the Bargello or perhaps the tale of "The Speaking Statues of the Via Cerratani."

Photograph by Alinari.

General Gattamelata, Padua, by Donatello.

They listened most eagerly. The story of the statues that spoke was their favorite and went like this:

There was once in Florence a young artist of great genius named Florio. He made marvelous works in bronze and marble, which were sold for high prices; and yet he was miserably poor. Still he wasted no money; and, far from having any vices, he lived like a modest saint. But as the saying is, "Whom God loveth, him He chasteneth!"

The secret of Florio's poverty was this: while he was still apprenticed to a very famous artist named Fabiano, the master, who was very shrewd, saw the youth's talent. Fabiano, therefore, made an agreement that for a certain sum which he was to receive monthly, Florio should bind himself to work for Fabiano, give him all he made, and swear to keep the secret that he had made the things which he had been set to do. And for a long time Florio was rejoiced at having made such a bargain.

But ere long it came to pass that for every hundred pounds that was paid to Florio for his work, Fabiano received a thousand and also got the credit for work which was far beyond his own power to perform.

And Florio was too honest to break the contract which he had made as a boy with a crafty master who had rightly judged of what was in him.

And this is a saying which may be found in Florence to the present day: that "the peasant killed the boar, and his lord got the credit of it." Yet all hidden things come to light, and all foxes meet some day at the furrier's.

Now there was a very learned and wise gentleman, one experienced in magic, named Simone; and it befell one day that he and many more gentlemen with ladies met at the studio of Fabiano to examine a marvelous bronze statue which the artist insisted was the best he had ever made; and those who had seen it declared it would be famous throughout Italy from A to Z. Nor was Fabiano backward in commending his own work. But the Signore Simone, who knew the truth, could not help pitying Florio when he saw him standing aside neglected, while Fabiano took all the thanks and all the compliments. At last, seeing the young man turn pale and red, and then, unobserved as he thought, wipe away a tear of grief, he resolved to aid him.

"Yes," remarked Fabiano, "it is not for me to praise my own work, but it is a fact that the Grand Duke said to me yesterday that all this statue wanted to be perfect was the gift of speech. But ah! art is difficult, and the trouble which I had to make it is beyond belief. If it could indeed speak, it would tell you marvelous, wondrous things."

"Per Bacco!" cried Simone, "thou sayest that in a good place and time. For I have learned in an old magic book an incantation which, when duly sung, will bring true speech to any statue's tongue, or to its lips if a tongue be wanting."

"Let us see the miracle by all means," exclaimed the Grand Duke.

"Let us hear, Simone!" cried the ladies.

Then Simone, speaking very solemnly, said:

> "By all the gods that once did dwell
> In every stream and tree,
> Open thy bronze lips; and like a bell,
> The secret of thy maker, tell."

Then the statue answered:

> "I was made by Florio.
> His the labor and the woe.
> At his sore toil he groweth old,
> While Fabiano gath'reth gold."

Dancing Children, the Cantoria, Florence, by Donatello

Photograph by Alinari.

Photograph by Alinari.

The Cantoria, Florence, by Donatello.

And all the statues in the room raised their brazen voices and called:

" 'Twas Florio made us, none but he.
To Florio let the glory be!"

Then the Grand Duke, being indignant at such injustice, ordered all this to be looked into. And when the whole truth came to light, it was decreed that the compact between Fabiano and Florio be broken and that the younger artist be allowed to take for his own all the works in his master's studio which he had made. And thus Florio became prosperous and famous, while Fabiano sank into merited contempt.

From which we may learn that "He who pastures his sheep in another man's field will some day lose all the flock," and:

He who sleeps in the devil's bed
By the devil will be awakenèd.

All the children would laugh exultantly to have Fabiano so outdone. And they would shake their heads sagely, saying: "If your statues could talk, O Donatello, they would speak honestly enough of their master. We have seen you at work upon them both day and night. We know!"

[114]

The Pipers, the Cantoria, by Donatello.

Photograph by Alinari.

Perhaps it was these children at his table; perhaps it was the crowds of boys and girls he saw playing hide-and-seek at dusk along the winding streets of Florence, who became the children of his "Bacchanal" of the pulpit at Prato and of his Singing Gallery or Cantoria made for the cathedral of Florence. No one knows, but at any rate in the Singing Gallery for the cathedral, in the "Bacchanal," and on the pulpit, Donatello made such boys and girls as have never been seen in the world before, romping, full of mischief, gay, and all of them singing fit to split their cheeks. He made, too, the grave little St. John, so full of long thoughts. And such merry rogues, *putti*, the Italians called them! They are all of them full of mischief, full of joy as young goats. They are Donatello's children, more famous than ever his living children could have been.

With these children of his clever hand, Donatello passed his old age cheerfully; and when he could no longer work, he was cared for by the great Cosimo de Medici. And after the death of Cosimo, by that generous man's wish, his son Piero continued to care for Donatello. Piero bestowed on him a farm. At first Donatello was delighted; " . . . but," writes the Old Historian, "he had held the property not more than a year before he came to Messer Piero, declaring that he could not have his quiet disturbed by thinking of household cares and listening to the troubles and outcries of the farmers, who came pestering him every third day, now because the wind had unroofed the dove-cote, now because the cattle had been seized for taxes, and anon because of the storms which had cut up the fruit trees!" He was so completely worn out, he continued, that "he would rather perish with hunger than be tormented by so many cares!" Piero laughed at the simplicity of Donatello, and to free him of all his troubles took the farm back and placed a sum of even greater value in the bank of Florence, where Donatello could draw upon it at his will. This brought gayety indeed to the sculptor, and he found life good. He was famous all over Italy and in other lands as well; and his good friend Brunelleschi had crowned the cathedral with its great dome and made himself one of the mightiest builders of all time.

And so now Donatello could sit all day resting after his long, busy life, resting and dreaming of his Zuccone and of his *putti*, made of bronze and marble, his merry children with their small heads full of tricks.

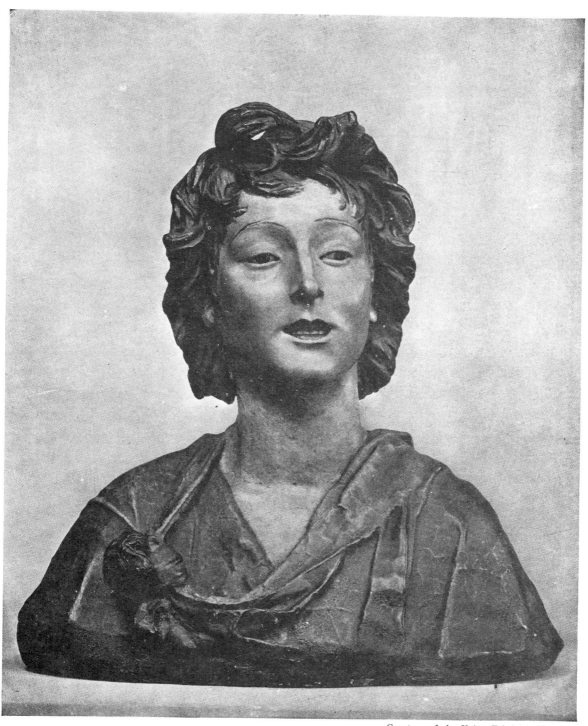

The Young John the Baptist, by Donatello.

The Secret A Bambino keeps Della Robbia

THE SECRET A BAMBINO KEEPS

Although the father and grandfather of Luca della Robbia were both shoemakers, he was sent to learn the trade of a goldsmith from the best goldsmith in the city of Florence, the aged Leonardo di Ser Giovanni. But the boy had greater ambitions even than this. The brightness of jewels, the gleam of gold, the rainbow hues of the enamels which he made, were dull and heavy in his eyes. To place a great milky pearl in a setting as fine as lacework, yet strong and well fashioned; to form a goblet for the banquet table of a prince; to chase upon a silver platter vines and flower petals so beautifully drawn that they appeared to grow, all seemed to the young Luca but child's play. He wanted to become a sculptor and carve from marble beautiful figures such as he loved to look at in the churches and large public buildings of Florence. He worked hard and won great success. At last in 1446, he was able to buy a house on the Via Guelpha, where he lived with his two nephews, Simone and Andrea, whom he adopted. Simone followed his father and grandfather and became a shoemaker, but Andrea studied with his uncle Luca and became an artist.

Now the house on the Via Guelpha was what is known to the Italians as a *bottega*. It was half a place where the artist worked, that is, a studio, and half a place where the artist sold his goods, a shop. There a man might go and order a statue as one would order a coat or a dress. There did Luca della Robbia make his own beautiful figures; there he taught Andrea and other young workers; there he re-discovered, or used in a new way, an art for which all Italy soon began to praise him. He not only made his figures out of marble, but he began to make them out of baked clay or terra cotta. This he covered with a beautiful shining creamy-white surface called a glaze of enamel. The glaze, like glass, was made first of all of melted sand which was mixed with molten lead and tin. The tin was important and made this kind of glaze different from all others. The white glaze coated the entire terra cotta figure.

Next the figure was covered with colored glazes. Then it was put into the ovens a second time and baked. Luca della Robbia used only a few colors: blue, yellow, green, and touches of violet. The paint had to be put on with an absolutely sure

The Cymbal Players, the Cantoria, by Luca della Robbia.

hand; not a moment of waiting, not a chance to re-touch, or the color would appear uneven, would run or smear.

The story of this kind of tin glaze is a long one and has its beginnings far in the eastern part of the world. No one is quite sure what people first discovered the secret; but it came probably from the land of Persia, the country of bright tiles, rich cloths, spices, weapons inlaid with gold, and peacock-colored pottery. The Arabs, being a wandering people, perhaps fell in with some Persian potter who taught them the art. Tiles on their buildings show us that they long held the secret of the glaze.

The Arabs in turn passed the knowledge on to the people of Europe, probably through trading and bargaining, just as they taught the Europeans to write the numbers that we use to-day. The Spanish were perhaps the first Europeans to make use of this glaze. They used tiles in all their buildings; and with glazed tiles the Moors decorated one building which has been for centuries a bright dream to all Europe, the palace of the Alhambra. The fame of this building spread, as did the fame of their pottery, dishes, bowls, plates. The island of Majolica was especially noted for its ware, and from this island came the name Majolica that is used to-day for pottery with a glaze of tin enamel.

Italian potters had known glazed pottery for years, but it was Luca della Robbia in Italy who first made use of the brilliant tin glaze with which he covered his figures. He may have fallen in with some wandering Moorish potter from Spain and improved upon the suggestions thus received. Or, by constant experimentation, he may have worked out alone, without help, a glaze similar to that known to the ancient rulers of Spain.

It was the art of modeling terra cotta figures and of glazing and painting them which Luca della Robbia worked at in his *bottega*. It must have taken years of struggle and trial before he was able to get just the shade he desired for his glaze, like old ivory or thick clotted cream. His colors were hard to manage too, since before they were put in the ovens for the final baking, they looked very different from the way that we see them now, green being gray until it was baked, and all the colors dark and muddy until they felt the heat. He could not see his colors; he had to know them.

In the Via Guelpha he taught Andrea, his nephew, who was a clever, willing pupil and who worked side by side with his uncle for many years. So closely did they work one with the other that it is difficult sometimes to tell whether this saint or that Madonna is the work of Luca or of the young Andrea. Simone lived with them, but always he busied himself at the cobbler's bench. At length when after a long life

Madonna and Child, by Luca della Robbia.

Alleluia Group, the Cantoria, by Luca della Robbia.

The Trumpeters, the Cantoria, by Luca della Robbia.

as one of the best-known of the Italian artists, Luca della Robbia died, he left his fortune and all his goods to his nephew Simone. For he said that while he had taught Andrea his art, he had never taught Simone anything. The art that Andrea had learned was a greater thing than are houses and lands, and so he said: "I do no injustice when I leave all my gold to Simone since I have given all my wisdom to Andrea."

Andrea continued to live in the house on the Via Guelpha. He lived a simple, hard-working life as had his uncle before him, and was soon surrounded with a large family of black-eyed children. There were twelve of them:.Antonia, Marco, Giovanni, Paolo, Lisabetta, Luca, Francesco, Caterina, Piero, Margherita, Girolamo, and Maria. Wherever you hear of the work of Andrea della Robbia, however learned may be the books in which you read of him, you will aways find it said that his figures of little children are among the most beautiful things that he made. Possibly the reason may lie in those twelve names. If he wanted to model a fat cheek, a round fist, curls, a smile, a pout, he had but to call Marco, Girolamo, Luca, or Lisabetta. Very probably many of the little figures which he placed on altars—angels and young saints—were but portraits of those twelve growing up around him.

When Andrea was not more than twenty-eight, he received a very important order. He was commissioned to make decorations for the porch or loggia of the Foundling Hospital in Florence. To this hospital little orphaned babies were and still are taken to be cared for by the good nuns. Andrea made a series of round plaques colored a beautiful blue in which were modeled little figures, *bambini* (babies) wrapped in swaddling clothes. Each *bambino* is really like a portrait of some particular child. One is serious, one wistful; one is roguish, one merry, one a little sad. All hold out their hands not to beg, but as if to ask quietly that the passer-by be so kind as to remember the children within, the children of the poor who have neither home nor parents, and who but for the nuns would fare miserably indeed.

From the time when he finished the *bambini,* Andrea was busy almost day and night working on decorations for churches and hospitals, monasteries and convents. He, like his uncle, Luca della Robbia, had a group of young men who worked with him and learned to make the clay figures and to cover them with colored glazes.

Under the skillful touch of Andrea, Florence grew bright with little figures (*putti*); altars were put up in the churches; arches were placed above doorways. Rich men and nobles sought Andrea to decorate their palaces. There were tall figures of St. Francis, who tamed the wolf of Gubbio; there were gentle Madonnas bending above the Christmas Child; there were portraits of men and little children. Not only in Florence but all over Italy the name of Andrea della Robbia was spoken. Orders came from north and south, east and west. Andrea, like his uncle, Luca della Robbia, lived long, and was known as one of the great artists of his time.

But finally, when he had left the *bottega* on the Via Guelpha forever, the days that followed were not so good for those who were left behind. The saying goes that when Andrea went away an evil spirit entered. However that may be, it is certain that, as the years went on, so busy became the shop, so many the orders, so hurried the workers, that no longer were the figures so carefully modeled as they had been, no longer was the color so fresh, or the glaze like white satin grown a little old.

People wondered at the change, and they said: "Surely Luca and his nephew had some great secret which they have kept from all the world." Soon the folk of Florence and other towns of Italy began to wonder where the secret could be hidden, the secret of the creamy glaze, of the bright colors. Some one answered the question, saying: "Perhaps Luca, or Andrea of the quick hand, wrote it on a parchment and hid it." But where could he have put the parchment on which were written such precious words? Another answered: "Perhaps the secret is within one of the statues." A great many people took up the word, and the legend or story grew, passed from man to woman, from boy to girl. Finally one said: "Surely Andrea knew the secret. It lay with him. It would surely be in Florence that he hid it. He would have put it high above the reach of ordinary men."

The *bambini* on the foundling hospital smiled down on all the curious crowd. They held out their hands quietly, with a kind of invitation in their open palms. Surely they were wise *bambini*. Perhaps they knew. That was it! All Florence took up the word. "The secret of the glaze is hidden on a parchment somewhere back of one of the *bambini*." They looked at the merriest one. "He is happy because he knows." They looked at the roguish one. "He is laughing because we have forgotten." They looked at the wistful baby. "He would like to tell us." They looked at the sad *bambino*. "He is sorry for all the beauty which left the world when Luca and Andrea della Robbia ceased to make the angels for our altars, the saints for our monasteries." But no one ever found out which baby kept the secret or what it was, though there were some who even longed to break the *bambini* to find out what it was they knew.

A Bambino, by Andrea della Robbia, from the Foundling Hospital.

A Bambino from the Foundling Hospital, by Andrea della Robbia.

It is not a good thing to question much about old folk-tales and legends, but if you could ask the great Luca or Andrea what secret it is the *bambino* keeps they would perhaps tell you that the secret could never be written on parchment. All the artists of Italy knew how to make the glaze; both Luca and Andrea had talked of it freely. *There was no secret* except that of long days and late nights of toil. It had to do only with working over the clay; with mixing the glaze honestly and painstakingly; with color ground slowly and well; with careful firing; and putting on the terra cotta swiftly and surely. The secret is nothing but what all true artists know. It is work, everlasting and unending. Luca della Robbia, toiling all night with his feet in a basket of shavings to keep them from freezing, knew it. Andrea with his careful modeling knew it. Later artists who made altar-pieces but to sell them and rushed on to make others and yet more forgot the secret of work, and so the knowledge of their art has grown dim. But the *bambini,* made with care and thought, do indeed hold that secret, not as the old tale goes, written on a parchment; but they keep it in every carefully modeled line, in the bright clear blue of the background, in the smooth glaze, in the little faces that look down on all the passers-by going to and fro along the dusty streets f Florence.

Bust of a Boy, by Andrea della Robbia.

THE GOLDSMITH
✠ OF FLORENCE ✠
CELLINI

THE GOLDSMITH OF FLORENCE

Fifty-four years had passed since the death of Brunelleschi, forty-five since Ghiberti had put aside his last tool, thirty-four since Donatello had ceased to carve, and eighteen since the hour when the aged Luca della Robbia began his last long sleep. It was the year fifteen hundred, as one night Master Giovanni Cellini walked back and forth across the rooms of his house, his eyes upon the ground, his hands clasped behind him. A good neighbor appeared at the door, carrying a tiny, swaddled *bambino*. Trembling with excitement, the master took the child into his arms; and when he heard the words that told him it was a son who had that night been born to him, his delight knew no bounds. "Joining together the palms of his old hands, he raised them, with his eyes, to God, and said: 'Lord, I thank Thee with my whole heart; this gift is very dear to me; let him be Welcome.' All the persons who were there asked him joyfully what name the child should bear. Giovanni would make no other answer than 'Let him be Welcome—Benvenuto'; and so they resolved, and this name was given me at Holy Baptism, and by it I still am living with the grace of God." *

So did Benvenuto, who was called "Welcome," tell the story of his birth and of his name. This and much more he wrote down in the history of his life. The story is one of the immortal stories of all the world. It is crammed with adventure, both good and bad, full of tales both false and true, of deeds both kind and treacherous; but it is always bright with bravery, laughter, and singing, and bubbling to the brim with life.

Benvenuto's dangerous adventures began when he was young indeed. He writes, "Andrea Cellini [his grandfather] was yet alive when I was about three years old and he had passed his hundredth. One day they had been altering a certain conduit pertaining to a cistern, and there issued from it a great scorpion unperceived by them, which crept down from the cistern to the ground, and slank away beneath a bench. I saw it, and ran to it and laid my hands upon it. It was so big that when I had it in my little hands, it put out its tail on one side, and on the

* All the quotations in this story are from "The Life of Benvenuto Cellini Written by Himself."

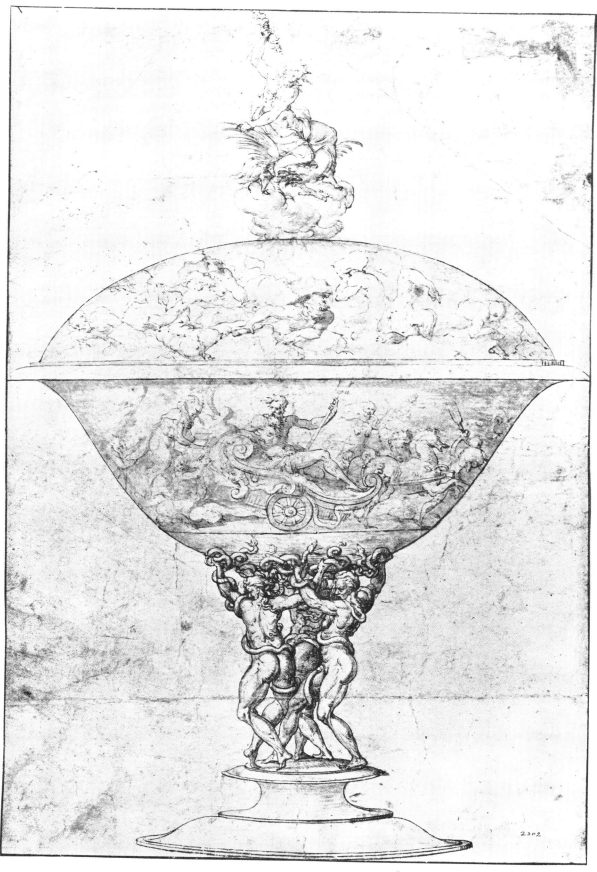

A Design for a Cup, attributed to Cellini.

other thrust forth both its mouths. They relate that I ran in high joy to my grand-father, crying, 'Look, Grandpapa, at my pretty crab!'

"When he recognized that the creature was a scorpion, he was on the point of falling dead for the great fear he had and anxiety about me. He coaxed and entreated me to give it him; but the more he begged, the tighter I clasped it, crying, and saying I would not give it to any one. My father, who was also in the house, ran up when he heard my screams and in his stupefaction could not think how to prevent the venomous animal from killing me. Just then his eyes chanced to fall upon a pair of scissors; and so while soothing and caressing me, he cut its tail and mouths off. Afterwards, when the great peril had been thus averted, he took the occurrence for a good augury."

Benvenuto was very little older when he saw the first of many marvels and miracles. "When I was about five years old, my father happened to be in a basement-chamber of our house, where they had been washing and where a good fire of oak-logs was still burning; he had a viol in his hand and was playing and singing alone beside the fire. The weather was very cold. Happening to look into the fire, he spied in the middle of those most burning flames a little creature like a lizard, which was sporting in the core of the intensest coals. Becoming instantly aware of what the thing was, he had my sister and me called, and pointing it out to us children, gave me a great box on the ears, which caused me to howl and weep with all my might. Then he pacified me good-humoredly and spoke as follows: 'My dear little boy, I am not striking you for any wrong that you have done, but only to make you remember that that lizard which you see in the fire is a sala-mander, a creature which has never been seen before by any one of whom we have credible information.' So saying, he kissed me and gave me some pieces of money."

The viol that Messer Giovanni Cellini had beside him in the basement-chamber of his house caused his son much displeasure. Being a musician himself, the father made up his mind that Benvenuto should also become one. Benvenuto cared much more about drawing and painting. ". . . I entreated him," writes Benvenuto, "to let me draw a certain fixed number of hours in the day; all the rest of my time I would give to music, only with the view of satisfying his desire. Upon this he said to me: 'So then, you take no pleasure in playing?' To which I answered, 'No'; because that art seemed too base in comparison with what I had in my own mind. My good father, driven to despair by this fixed idea of mine, placed me in the workshop of . . . Michel Agnolo, a goldsmith . . . and a master

The Castle of Sant' Angelo, Rome, from which Cellini escaped during his adventures in Rome.

Photograph by Alinari.

excellent in that craft. After I had stayed there some days, my father took me away from Michel Agnolo, finding himself unable to live without having me always under his eyes. Accordingly, much to my discontent, I remained at music till I reached the age of fifteen.

"When I reached the age of fifteen, I put myself, against my father's will, to the goldsmith's trade with a man called Antonio, son of Sandro, known commonly as Marcone the Goldsmith. He was a most excellent craftsman and a very good fellow to boot, high-spirited and frank in all his ways. . . . My liking for the art was so great, or, I may truly say, my natural bias, both one and the other, that in a few months I caught up the good, nay, the best young craftsmen in our business, and began to reap the fruits of my labors. I did not, however, neglect to gratify my good father from time to time by playing on the flute or cornet. Each time he heard me I used to make his tears fall, accompanied with deep-drawn sighs of satisfaction."

So did Benvenuto enter upon his two accomplishments, the one which he loathed, the other that he loved with all his heart. They seem like quite peaceful occupations, but Cellini's life was continuously warlike. Having got mixed up in a brawl, he was banished from Florence and sent to Rome. In Rome, however, he quickly found both work and friends.

So skillfully did he do his work that he was summoned by Pope Clement to make various pieces of jewelry for him. Having traveled back and forth to Florence many times, Benvenuto finally set up a shop in Rome. It was here that he had one of his most exciting experiences. "The Pope had sent me all those precious stones. . . . I had five excellent journeymen, and in addition to the great piece [the "great piece" was a large button for the Pope's cope], I was engaged on several jobs; so that my shop contained a property of much value in gems, and gold and silver. I kept a shaggy dog, very big and handsome, which Duke Alessandro gave me; the beast was capital as a retriever, since he brought me every sort of bird and game I shot, but he also served most admirably for a watchdog.

" . . . My slumber is sometimes very deep and heavy. So it chanced one night: for I must say that a thief, under the pretext of being a goldsmith, had spied on me and cast his eyes upon the precious stones and made a plan to steal them. Well, then, this fellow broke into the shop, where he found a quantity of little things in gold and silver. He was engaged in bursting open certain boxes to get at the jewels he had noticed, when my dog jumped upon him and put him to much trouble to defend himself with his sword. The dog, unable to grapple with an armed man, ran several times through the house and rushed into the rooms of the journeymen, which had been left open because of the great heat. When he found they paid no heed to his loud barking, he dragged their bedclothes off; and when they still heard nothing, he pulled first one and then another by the arm till he roused them and, barking furiously, ran before to show them where he wanted them to go. At last it became clear that they refused to follow, for the traitors, cross at being disturbed, threw stones and sticks at him; and this they could well do, for I had ordered them to keep all night a lamp alight there; and in the end they shut their rooms tight; so the dog, abandoning all hope of aid from such rascals, set out alone again on his adventure. He ran down, and not finding the thief in the shop, flew after him. When he got at him, he tore the cape off his back. It would have gone hard with the fellow had he not called for help to certain tailors, praying them for God's sake to save him from a mad dog; and they, believing what he said, jumped out and drove the dog off with much trouble.

"After sunrise my workmen went into the shop and saw that it had been broken open and all the boxes smashed. They began to scream at the top of their voices: 'Ah, woe is me! Ah, woe is me!' The clamor woke me, and I rushed out in a panic. Appearing thus before them, they cried out: 'Alas to us! for we have been robbed by some one who has broken and borne everything away!' These words wrought so forcibly upon my mind that I dared not go to my big chest and look if it still held the jewels of the Pope. So intense was the anxiety that I seemed to lose my eyesight and told them they themselves must unlock the chest and see how many of the Pope's gems were missing.

"The fellows were all in their shirts; and when, on opening the chest, they saw the precious stones and my work with them, they took heart of joy and shouted: 'There is no harm done; your piece and all the stones are here; but the thief has left us naked to the shirt, because last night, by reason of the burning heat, we took our clothes off in the shop and left them here.' Recovering my senses, I thanked God, and said: 'Go and get yourselves new suits of clothes; I will pay when I hear at leisure how the whole thing happened.'"

So did Benvenuto's dog save the Pope's jewels. One cannot but wonder if the beautiful plaque which Cellini made of a dog might not perhaps have been modeled in grateful remembrance of this brave animal.

Having undergone one tremendous experience after another, among them a lengthy service under the king of France, Benvenuto came again to Florence in the year 1545. The Duke of Florence was Cosimo de Medici, a descendant of that great

Photograph by Alinari.

A Bronze Relief of a Dog, attributed to Cellini.

Cosimo for whom Donatello had worked. The Duke commissioned Cellini to make for him, not a gem or a tiny silver or golden figure, but a large statue in bronze. The figure was to be Perseus, who slew the Gorgon with her snaky locks. Benvenuto made a model in wax which he brought to the Duke. "After having well considered it for some time, always with greater satisfaction, he [the Duke] began as follows: 'If you could only execute this little model, Benvenuto, with the same perfection on a large scale, it would be the finest piece in the Piazza.' I replied: 'Most excellent my lord, upon the Piazza are now standing works by the great Donatello and the incomparable Michelangelo, the two greatest men who have ever lived since the days of the ancients. But since your Excellence encourages my model with such praise, I feel the heart to execute it at least thrice as well in bronze.' Being now inflamed with a great desire to begin working, I told his Excellency that I had need of a house where I could install myself and erect furnaces in order to commence operations in clay and bronze, and also, according to their separate requirements, in gold and silver. While the workshop for executing my Perseus was in building, I used to work in the ground-floor room. Here I modeled the statue in plaster, giving it the same dimensions as the bronze was meant to have, and intending to cast it from this mold."

Many things both vexatious and pleasurable interfered with the work Benvenuto had in hand. One of his chief difficulties lay in the lack of skill of his assistants, at least that is what Benvenuto says about it. He writes: "Nevertheless I felt convinced that when my Perseus was accomplished, all these trials would be turned to high felicity and glorious well-being."

Now the modeling and casting of such a figure was indeed a great task. Benvenuto followed in general the same process that Ghiberti used years before when he cast the bronze gates for the Baptistry. Benvenuto made his Perseus in clay somewhat roughly. When it was finished, he covered it with a layer of wax modeled very carefully, for from it the finished work would take its form. Over the wax was put a mold or matrix, that is, the wax was covered by a paste made of pounded brick, ashes, and clay mixed with water until it was about the thickness of cream. This was pressed very carefully into all the little curves of the wax. It was called by Benvenuto not mold or matrix, but the "clay tunic." When it had dried, as even greater protection for the work within, more clay was packed on the outside until the figure looked rather like a shapeless lump of rock with the jewel hidden away inside. To hold all in place, the outer layer was securely bound with bands of iron. Vent pipes had to be put through the outer molds, and "tunic," some to let out the wax when it should melt, some to allow heat and steam to escape.

When all this first part of the work was done, the figure was put in the furnace where the clay wrappings were baked until they were entirely hard. At the same time, of course, the wax melted away, leaving a hollow where it had been. Into this space the melted bronze was to be poured. Bronze is a combination of copper and tin, with certain other metals called alloys used in small quantities. These must be mixed in correct proportions to the whole or the bronze will cake and curdle instead of liquefy with the heat. When, after perhaps a week of waiting, the figure had cooled, it was unearthed from its outer walls, polished, burnished, and retouched here and there with a clever tool. And that which a few days before had been of crumbling clay was now made lasting for all the ages. Benvenuto tells with what great labor, pains, and terror he cast the Perseus.

"Accordingly I strengthened my heart, and with all the forces of my body and my purse, employing what little money still remained to me, I set to work. First, I provided myself with several loads of pine-wood. . . . While these were on their way, I clothed my Perseus in clay which I had prepared many months beforehand, in order that it might be duly seasoned. After making its clay tunic (for that is the term used in this art) and properly arming it and fencing it with iron girders, I began to draw the wax out by means of a slow fire. This melted and issued through numerous air-vents I had made; for the more of these there are, the better will the mold fill. When I had finished drawing off the wax, I constructed a funnel-shaped furnace all round the model of my Perseus. It was built of bricks, so interlaced, the one above the other, that numerous apertures were left for the fire to exhale at. Then I began to lay on wood by degrees, and kept it burning two whole days and nights.

"At length when all the wax was gone and the mold was well baked, I set to work at digging the pit in which to sink it. This I performed with scrupulous regard to all the rules of art. When I had finished that part of my work, I raised the mold by windlasses and stout ropes to a perpendicular position, and suspending it with the greatest care one cubit above the level of the furnace so that it hung exactly above the middle of the pit, I next lowered it gently down into the very bottom of the furnace, and had it firmly placed with every possible precaution for its safety. When this delicate operation was accomplished, I began to bank it up with the earth I had excavated; and, ever as the earth grew higher, I introduced its proper air-vents, which were little tubes of earthenware, such as folks use for drains and such-like purposes. At length, I felt sure that it was admirably fixed, and that the filling-in of the pit and the placing of the air-vents had been properly performed. I also could see that my work-people understood my method, which differed very considerably from that of all the other masters in the trade.

"Feeling confident, then, that I could rely upon them, I next turned to my furnace, which I had filled with numerous pigs of copper [masses of copper] and other bronze stuff. The pieces were piled according to the laws of art, that is to say, so resting one upon the other that the flames could play freely through them, in order that the metal might heat and liquefy the sooner. At last I called out heartily to set the furnace going. The logs of pine were heaped in, and, what with the unctuous resin of the wood and the good draught I had given, my furnace worked so well that I was obliged to rush from side to side to keep it going. The labor was more than I could stand; yet I forced myself to strain every nerve and muscle. To increase my anxieties, the workshop took fire, and we were afraid lest the roof should fall upon our heads; while from the garden such a storm of wind and rain kept blowing in, that it perceptibly cooled the furnace.

"Battling thus with all these untoward circumstances for several hours, and exerting myself beyond even the measure of my powerful constitution, I could at last

The Perseus, by Cellini.

bear up no longer, and a sudden fever, of the utmost possible intensity, attacked me. I felt absolutely obliged to go and fling myself upon my bed.

"No sooner had I got to bed (leaving my work-people to continue the casting) than I ordered my serving-maids to carry food and wine for all the men into the workshop; at the same time I cried: 'I shall not be alive to-morrow.' They tried to encourage me, arguing that my illness would pass over, since it came from excessive fatigue. In this way I spent two hours battling with fever, which steadily increased, and calling out continually: 'I feel that I am dying.' . . . While I was thus terribly afflicted, I beheld the figure of a man enter my chamber, twisted in his body into the form of a capital S. He raised a lamentable, doleful voice, like one who announces their last hour to men condemned to die upon the scaffold, and spoke these words: 'O Benvenuto, your statue is spoiled, and there is no hope whatever of saving it.' No sooner had I heard the shriek of that wretch than I gave a howl which might have been heard from the sphere of flame. Jumping from my bed, I seized my clothes and began to dress. The maids, and my lad, and every one who came around to help me got kicks, or blows of the fist, while I kept crying out in lamentation: 'Ah! traitors! enviers! This is an act of treason, done by malice prepense! But I swear by God that I will sift it to the bottom and before I die will leave such witness to the world of what I can do as shall make a score of mortals marvel!'

"When I had got my clothes on, I strode with soul bent on mischief toward the workshop; there I beheld the men, whom I had left erewhile in such high spirits, standing stupefied and downcast. I began at once and spoke: 'Up with you! Attend to me! Since you have not been able or willing to obey the directions I gave you, obey me now that I am with you to conduct my work in person. Let no one contradict me, for in cases like this we need the aid of hand and hearing, not of advice.' I went immediately to inspect the furnace and found that the metal was all curdled; an accident which we express by 'being caked.' I told two of the hands to cross the road and fetch from the house of the butcher Capretta a load of young oak-wood, which had lain dry for about a year; this wood had been previously offered me by Madame Ginevra, wife of the said Capretta. So soon as the first armfuls arrived, I began to fill the grate beneath the furnace. Now oak-wood of that kind heats more powerfully than any other sort of tree; and for this reason, where a slow fire is wanted, as in the case of gun-foundry, alder or pine is preferred. Accordingly, when the logs took fire, oh! how the cake began to stir beneath that awful heat, to glow and sparkle in a blaze! At the same time I

Palazzo Vecchio and Loggia dei Lanzi, Florence.
Cellini's Perseus stands in the Loggia.

Photograph by Alinari.

kept stirring up the channels and sent men upon the roof to stop the conflagration which had gathered force from the increased combustion in the furnace; also I caused boards, carpets, and other hangings to be set up against the garden, in order to protect us from the violence of the rain.

"When I had thus provided against these several disasters, I roared out first to one man and then to another: 'Bring this thing here! Take that thing there!' At this crisis, when the whole gang saw the cake was on the point of melting, they did my bidding, each fellow working with the strength of three. I then ordered half a pig of pewter to be brought, which weighed about sixty pounds, and flung it into the middle of the cake inside the furnace. By this means, and by piling on wood and stirring now with pokers and now with iron rods, the curdled mass rapidly began to liquefy. Then, knowing I had brought the dead to life again, against the firm opinion of those ignoramuses, I felt such vigor fill my veins that all those pains of fever, all those fears of death, were quite forgotten.

"All of a sudden an explosion took place, attended by a tremendous flash of flame, as though a thunderbolt had formed and then discharged amongst us. Unwonted and appalling terror astonished every one, and me more than the rest. When the din was over and the dazzling light extinguished, we began to look each other in the face. Then I discovered that the cap of the furnace had blown up, and the bronze was bubbling over from its source beneath. So I had the mouths of my mold immediately opened, and at the same time drove in two plugs which kept back the molten metal. But I noticed that it did not flow as rapidly as usual, the reason being probably that the fierce heat of the fire we kindled had consumed its base alloy. Accordingly I sent for all my pewter platters, porringers, and dishes, to the number of some two hundred pieces, and had a portion of them cast, one by one, into the channels, the rest into the furnace. This expedient succeeded, and every one could now perceive that my bronze was in most perfect liquefaction, and my mold was filling; whereupon they all with heartiness and happy cheer assisted and obeyed my bidding, while I, now here, now there, gave orders, helped with my own hands, and cried aloud: 'O God! Thou that by Thy immeasurable power didst rise from the dead, and in Thy glory didst ascend to heaven!' . . . even thus in a moment my mold was filled; and seeing my work finished, I fell upon my knees, and with all my heart gave thanks to God.

"After all was over, I turned to a plate of salad on a bench there, and ate with hearty appetite, and drank together with the whole crew. Afterwards I retired to bed, healthy and happy, for it was now two hours before morning, and slept

The Cellini Cup.

as sweetly as though I had never felt a touch of illness. My good housekeeper, without my giving any orders, had prepared a fat capon for my repast. So that, when I rose, about the hour for breaking fast, she presented herself with a smiling countenance, and said: 'Oh! is that the man who felt that he was dying? Upon my word, I think the blows and kicks you dealt us last night, when you were so enraged, and had that demon in your body as it seemed, must have frightened away your mortal fever! The fever feared that it might catch it too, as we did!' All my poor household, relieved in like measure from anxiety and overwhelming labor, went at once to buy earthen vessels in order to replace the pewter I had cast away. Then we dined together joyfully: nay, I cannot remember a day in my whole life when I dined with greater gladness or a better appetite."

In this manner was the Perseus cast. It was the crowning deed of the worker's life and won him no little fame. The rest of his days were spent quietly at his workbench in Florence. Among the many beautiful objects made by Cellini is the cup now in the Altman Collection of the Metropolitan Museum of Art. The body of the cup is a beautiful gold enamel; the bands of floral decoration, greens, rose, and crimson. The body of the siren which decorates the cup is gold; her tail is of iridescent green scales. The scales of the dragon which holds up the cup are of a slightly darker, jewel-like green; the turtle is sparkling orange and black. Nothing but a long look at the cup can give an idea of its brilliant richness and the marvel of skill that went into the making of the minutest scroll, the setting of the smallest jewel.

Little wonder that he was known as the greatest goldsmith in the city of his birth; little wonder, too, that he was called its merriest teller of tales. He had rightly earned the name which years before Master Giovanni Cellini gave to him when he said: "Lord, I thank Thee with my whole heart; this gift is very dear to me; let him be Welcome—Benvenuto!"

DURING THE REVOLUTION, — AND NOW A FOREWORD

In those troubled days when the American Colonies were growing into a nation, there were a number of men who kept the spirit and beauty of the Old World alive in the New, even while they were fighting for freedom from outworn manners, customs, and governments. Among these men, artists and craftsmen, was Paul Revere. He forms a sort of bridge between the Europe which this book has so far been considering and the world of to-day. He was not only a messenger riding from Boston Town to Lexington and Concord, but also a messenger carrying the ideas of fine workmanship from the old times on to now.

The last two chapters tell of two men who received this message, and who, in the midst of the whirl of machines and the cries of "rush, rush," work slowly and carefully and with respect for their task. They are busy with chisel and hammer even as the reader turns the pages of this book. They are carrying on the great adventure of fine craftsmanship here, to-day.

BOSTON'S HANDYMAN
PAUL REVERE

BOSTON'S HANDYMAN

In the stormy and turbulent days when Henry III of France was on the throne, the court was much under the influence of the Dukes of Guise. Hither and yon these noblemen drove those whose ideas of religion did not agree with their own. And if the unfortunates were unable to escape, they suffered persecutions of a grievous kind. Among the many French Huguenots or Protestants who left France during this reign of fear was a family known as De Rivoire. They had been a family of power, and the ruins of a chateau occupied by them were visited by one of their descendants as late as the year 1875. It was situated in the southeastern part of France near the city of Vienne on the River Rhône.

England and Holland sheltered some of the fleeing Rivoires while others went to the island of Guernsey in the English Channel. Simon de Rivoire was among those who settled on the island. There, a young nephew was sent to him, Apollon, born in the year 1702, whose parents had managed to remain safely in a remote part of France. When the lad was not more than fourteen or fifteen, Simon sent him across the wide, gray seas to the American city of Boston. It was a long, lonely journey, beset with gales; but the boy, from all that is known of him, seems to have been a sturdy fellow and to have taken his luck as a man among men. He went to the new world to seek his fortune and to learn the trade of silversmith. This he did well, for although his master died before the boy had finished his apprenticeship, yet he had progressed so well that he was an able and skilled craftsman.

After a visit to his relatives in Guernsey he decided to make Boston his home. The very first thing he did on his return to that city was to change his name "merely on account the Bumpkins should pronounce it better." He called himself Revere, a word which the English-speaking tongue could master easily. As soon as Apollon—now Apollo—had established himself in business, he married Miss Deborah Hitchborn. Soon the house was filled with small Reveres, all hardy and boisterous. Among them, the third of twelve boys and girls, was a son named Paul. He was born on January first, 1734.

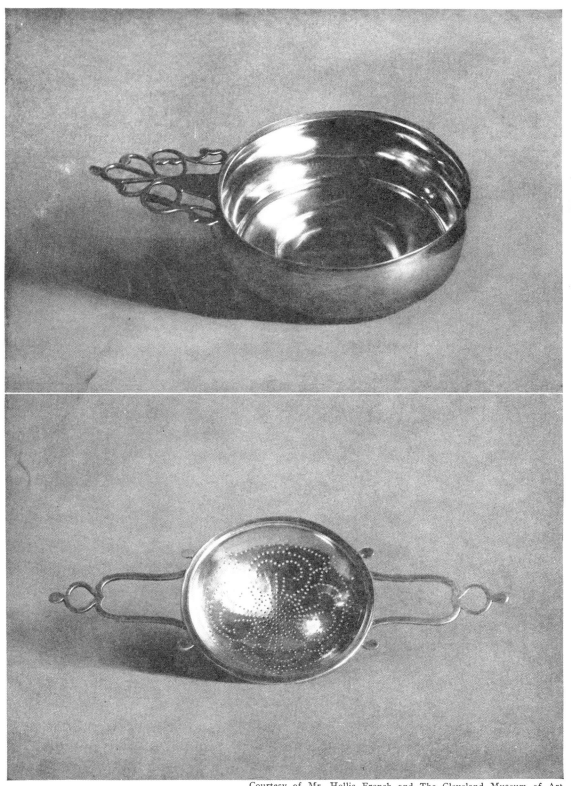

Courtesy of Mr. Hollis French and The Cleveland Museum of Art.

A Silver Porringer and a Strainer, by Paul Revere.

This Paul was a large child for his age and very active. He could scramble about in the woods with the best of them, was a good shot, could ride well, knew where the nuts were first ripe in the fall, the ice was thickest for skating in the winter, the pool clearest for bathing in the spring. Like all the small urchins in the Colony he was sent to school. He went to Master John Tileston, who was a schoolmaster for eighty years in Boston and far-famed for his teaching of penmanship. Paul learned to write a good hand and could figure quickly and easily, but he was never very well versed in the art of spelling, as his later letters show.

The schools in the Colonies often consisted of one room, large and bare, with a big stove in the center and the teacher's desk at one end. The building was often of logs and was built on blocks about two and a half feet above the ground, the space underneath making a fine meeting-place for hogs and chickens, who came rooting and pecking after bits of the children's lunch that might have dropped through wide cracks in the floor. In well-to-do Boston there may have been glass in the windows, but many of the schools had, instead of windowpanes, paper greased to make it translucent. The children had neither blackboards nor maps, though occasionally a globe. Slates were not used in Paul Revere's day; even the tiniest child had to struggle with pen and ink. The pens were goose quills, and the teacher had to be mending them continually.

In getting their paper ready for use, the children had to rule it themselves with a lead plummet, for there were no lead pencils in those days. These plummets were merely pieces of sheet lead, though sometimes the lead was melted and run into a wooden mold and later shaped out with a jackknife. The children liked them best in the form of tomahawks and often brandished them fiercely behind Master Tileston's back. Such mischief was, on the whole, not very safe. Master Tileston frequently applied the ruler to plump palms; the whipping-post was sometimes used. It was nothing to see a lad thrown across the master's knee while the birch rod fell in rhythmical strokes upon his person. Paul Revere probably fared no better than the rest. He was high-spirited and not afraid—even of Master Tileston.

Paul did well enough at school, but it was at home, where he was free to use his powers of invention and his skill of hand, that he showed himself for the clever lad he was. When the great iron pot sprung a leak, it was Paul who fixed it; when his mother's spinning wheel refused to turn, it was Paul who somehow contrived to mend it. Over the backlog in a Colonial fireplace, about seven feet from the ground, was what is known as a back bar, a rod made of green wood

A Portrait of Mrs. John Greene, by John Singleton Copley, R.A.
The frame is said to have been made by Paul Revere.

on which the pots and pans were hung while their contents boiled merrily. Now occasionally even with careful watching the back bar would begin to char; and one day a whole meal would go spurting and sizzling into the ashes, pots and pans rolling this way and that. It was a disaster indeed. At such times there were cries to the left and right, "Paul, Paul Revere, the back bar—it's down! Come quickly!" And in a few moments a new one would be in place and things once more set to rights.

All the boys knew how to whittle. A great many household utensils were made of wood—spoons, bowls, and even plates. Paul was especially clever with his knife. Not content to make utensils plain, he would carve now and then a leaf pattern or a wreath of flowers. This work was usually done as the family sat about the fire at night. It was a gay time. The French Huguenots were a jollier set than were the gray-clad Puritans. The household rang with merriment and laughter; jokes were passed and good tales told. There was no fear of black punishments to come in the next world or of the evil effects of pleasure in this. Objects of beauty were even looked at with approval; and a gay ribbon, a ruffle, a flounce were matters for a smile rather than for a frown. Paul Revere was indeed fortunate in his ancestry and his home life.

When quite a little boy, he began to help his father, Apollo, the silversmith, as an apprentice about the shop; gradually he began to learn the trade himself. First of all he had to acquaint himself with the kind of designs that were wanted by the ladies of the Colony for tea sets, bowls, spoons, or sugar tongs. On the whole the silver was quite simple, its only form of decoration being an occasional initial or a delicate band of engraving. This simplicity was probably due to the fact that all of the adventurers on these new shores had turned their backs upon the luxury and extravagances of the courts of France and England.

Before he could take up the hammer or graver, young Paul had to prove his ability to draw. He had to be able to make the patterns of his tankards, pitchers, and cans; moreover, he had to be able to put down on paper the little floral designs which wound themselves about a bowl or mug. He must have been what is known as a natural draftsman. So far any one knows he had no instruction save that which he got from his father, Apollo; but to this informal teaching, he brought unusually keen powers of observation. He probably drew at his father's workbench or lying in front of the fire in the evenings, asking as he did so: "Is this all right? Would you make this curve sharper? How do you make a monogram out of the letters E and H?" Undoubtedly the good Apollo would answer with the wonderful patience that fathers seem endowed with—at times. And gradually, without quite realizing how it happened, Paul Revere had reached the point where he took up the hammer of the silversmith and in his free time made something of his own.

It seems unlikely, however, that when he did begin, his first piece was made of silver. That was too expensive material for green lads to experiment with. He probably started with a bit of copper, out of which—if he were able—he could form a pot or bowl. Very likely his first equipment was much like the one illustrated. His tools: a simple metal stake which he fastened securely in the vise at his workbench; two or three hammers; and later when he became more experienced, a graver. His materials: a flat sheet of copper.

First of all he marked on the sheet with a compass a circle of the size he de-

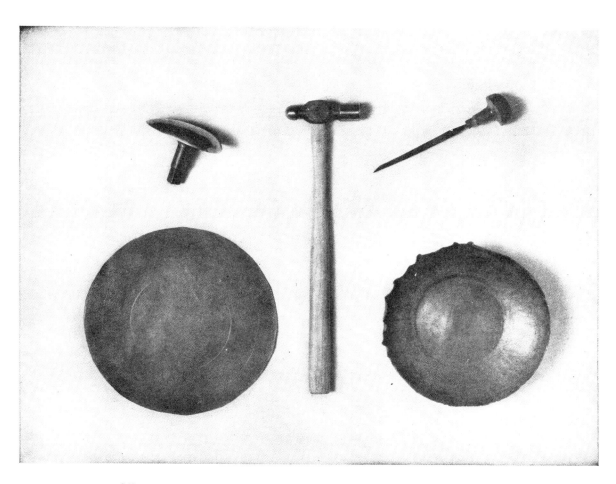

Silversmith's Tools and Copper Bowl in the Making.
Set prepared for The Cleveland Museum of Art by Anna Wÿers Hill, Silversmith.

sired; this circle he cut with a heavy pair of shears which could go through metal as easily as sewing-scissors through cloth. Then, also with his compass, he made two smaller circles, one to mark the area of the base of his bowl, the other to guide him as he hammered so that he would shape the bowl evenly. Taking his flat metal disk with the two circles engraved upon it, he held it against the stake and began to pound along the first circle. He found that by the time he had pounded round the bowl once his metal was so hard that he could no longer work upon it. Then it had to be put in the fire to be heated again, annealed, he called the process. This in itself was not so simple, for the metal had to be heated until it was red-hot.

If, by chance, he happened to heat his metal just the right degree, he began to pound around a second time. This step was not so simple either as it seemed when being performed by his father's deft hands. If he pounded too hard in one place the bowl would bulge so he could never get the unevenness hammered out; if he did not hammer hard enough, it refused to shape at all. And always just as he got things going well, he had to stop and anneal his material; this had to be done every time his hammer completed the circles of the bowl. When at last he did manage to persuade the bowl to show that it had a base, he hammered along the second circle, building up and rounding out the sides. He found that he was apt to get small scallops along the edges. This was all right if they were not too deep, but at times they became so decided that he found he could not beat them out; his bowl was permanently ruffled. No, it was not so easy!

Even though he had undoubted natural skill, it took months of steady practice before he was intrusted with a sheet of precious silver; and then he made only the simplest objects. He had learned by this time how to use the small metal stakes for rather sharply curved surfaces, the larger ones for a larger, more gentle curve. He had learned how to use the sharp-pointed graver and to make an initial or tiny pattern scratched or *engraved* upon the metal. This took a steady hand. A single mis-stroke and a beautiful surface was spoiled. And that must never happen.

The art of embossing was another kind of decoration that had to be mastered. Embossing tools are dull rather than pointed. Some of them are curved and can the more easily be used in making a scroll or petal-like pattern. The process of embossing is done on a pitchblock as is the process of embossing iron. The worker starts his design on the silver from the front; then, working from the back, he pushes it forward in relief. Yet often he has occasion to work from the front as he continues, especially in the stages of finishing. Young Paul discovered that in hammering at his embossing tool, it was very easy to hammer too hard. He was then in danger of going right through the metal. If he did not put enough pressure on his hammer, his tool made hardly any dent upon the surface at all; if he did not hammer evenly, he had "rabbit tracks," now a deep mark, now none, now a faint one. Hours and hours he spent on some simple design.

All of these difficulties were as nothing compared with the troubles he had with soldering. Solder is a metal or a combination of metals, or alloy, used when melted in joining metal surfaces. It is to metal what liquid glue is to wood. One day Paul Revere had so far progressed as to be intrusted with the making of a brass or pewter canister. This he had to cut out of a flat piece of the metal. To secure just the proper shape he hammered it a little over the stake and then soldered it together, usually making the seam at the point where the handle would later be attached. He used solder which would melt a little sooner than his copper. The moment he saw it melting, he had to snatch his burning torch away.

After several trials he could perhaps get his seam fairly well fitted. Then he would make the little rim that goes at the base. This was often, for the sake of the proper look and finish, made in several pieces and fastened together. A glance at the silver can illustrated will make this clear. When the ring was finished, it was slipped over the bottom of the can and soldered to it. Then a circle was cut just the right size to make the bottom. This in turn had to be soldered to the base. Then came the ring at the top. Now the handle had to be hammered out and soldered or riveted in place and the cover riveted or soldered to the ingenious little hinge that fastens it to the handle.

When Paul Revere had made his first can, he looked at it with all the pride in the world. It was a bit crooked in places. It looked rather like an old one instead of a new; it had nicks and marks here and there, where really they did not belong, but it was good and solid. "Now for the polishing," said Apollo. This was done on a wheel which was turned by means of a treadle. The wheel was first bound with a fine emery cloth and later with soft flannel or wool to give the piece its final shine. How his can gleamed in his hand! That was a day indeed. But would he ever be able to make a silver one?

Yes, and many of them. So beautiful were their designs and their workmanship that they are still being copied and probably always will be. Their shape and size are so well adapted to their use, their forms so beautiful, their surface polish so soft, that they cannot be improved upon. As for spoons and other flat tableware, all great concerns which make either silver or plated ware to-day are sure to find their

*A Tankard during the
process of soldering*

"Paul Revere Patterns" among the most beautiful and most popular. But the young man at his bench thought little of future fame. He had his work to do; do it he would with all the skill he could muster. This he resolved upon and no more. It was enough.

All the while that Paul Revere was growing up, the country was growing with him. Though it was still loyal in name to King George III and to England, there were many murmurs of discontent. The Whigs and Tories had heated arguments in which even the children took part. Many a young rebel came home from the schoolyard with a bleeding nose given him by a lusty Tory; many a young Tory had his long-tailed coat torn by the ruthless hand of a small Whig. When Paul was about sixteen, his father's workshop began to seem very quiet indeed. He became interested in military affairs; there were always border skirmishes going on

Courtesy of the Museum of Fine Arts, Boston.

A Silver Tankard, by Paul Revere.

between the Colonists and the Indians. When he was twenty-two, he had so far allied himself with the affairs of Massachusetts that he was made a lieutenant in the English army by General John Winslow. General Winslow was commanding an expedition against the French settlers who were in possession of disputed territory, Crown Point on Lake Champlain.

About this time the death of his father had a sobering effect on the young soldier; he had now to take charge of the shop and undertake to help bring up his father's family. He seems to have felt himself very competent in face of all this responsibility, for the next year, 1757, he married Miss Sarah Orne of Boston.

Soon he himself was the head of a growing household of children. The following years were taken up with his work of silversmith and with fitting himself for the clever mechanic which he later became. In May, 1773, his first wife died. Here he was with a growing family, the youngest nine months old and all "in sore need of a mother." He was not long in supplying this need, for in December of the same year he married Miss Rachel Walker, who remained his devoted helpmate until the very last years of his eventful life.

Though Paul Revere lived placidly enough in the sixteen years that carried him to the age of thirty-eight, much was happening in his country. The Stamp Act of 1765 had stirred the Colonists to fury. George III only increased the rage of the Americans by further imposing a tax on paper, painters' colors, glass, and tea. This was the far-off rumble of a war to come. But only one man knew it. The man who through all the anxiety, the uncertainty and doubt of the time, realized that a division must come between England and America was Samuel Adams. He and John Hancock became determined leaders in the quarrel that was brewing. As for most of the Colonists they were still loyal subjects of the crown, but they did not propose to be treated like children.

To Hancock and Adams and the group of men surrounding them Paul Revere attached himself, full of enthusiasm. He soon became the "express" for the "Sons of Liberty," a body of far-seeing men who held their meetings in The Green Dragon, a tavern kept by an ardent patriot. Paul Revere carried dispatches on his good horse. Leaving his workbench, he would gallop off along the rough, muddy roads to Philadelphia or to New York. These journeys were long and wearisome and required much of both man and horse.

Such interruptions in his work brought problems for the wage-earner of so large a family as that for which the hardy rider was now responsible; the fee he received as "express" was very small; and in order to keep clothes on the backs of the small Reveres and shoes on their feet, Paul turned to whatever he could, in order to gain a better livelihood. In his odd moments he practiced dentistry. The Boston *Gazette* of September 19, 1768, carried the following advertisement:

Whereas, many Persons are so unfortunate as to lose their foreteeth by Accident and otherways, to their great Detriment, not only in looks but speaking both in Public and Private. This is to inform all such that they may have them replaced with artificial Ones, that look as well as Natural and answers the end of speaking to all intents, by Paul Revere, Goldsmith, near the head of Dr. Clark's wharf, Boston.

The messenger of the Revolution continued this rather delicate trade for some time; it has even been said that he made a set of teeth for General Washington. But "pulling the teeth of the Redcoats" seems to have been more to his taste than repairing those of the Colonists. Even his skill at making engravings—drawings cut on copper-plate and printed therefrom—was turned in the direction of his country's affairs. By this process he was forever making cartoons and broadsides which kept the people of Boston alert and stirred as well as amused, perhaps. Now and then he would turn his talents to more peaceful channels and engrave a set of bookplates for some gentleman of the Colonies who was building up a library. These he did with no little skill and delicacy.

But the thing uppermost in his mind was the meetings at The Green Dragon. England had demanded that the House of Representatives of Massachusetts rescind (take back) certain demands they had made for further liberty. Ninety-two of the members of the House voted not to rescind and stood ready to take the consequences of their act. By way of congratulation the "Sons of Liberty" decided to present the ninety-two with a memorial of their bravery. They decided upon a silver punch-bowl. Who was to make it? None other than their "express," Paul Revere. This he did with great finish and skill. Historically, it is one of his most important works.

Whether with his hand upon his delicate graver or his foot in the stirrup, Paul Revere was busy about the affairs of his country. He was among those who planned and executed one of the most brilliant accomplishments of pre-Revolutionary days. The tax on tea became more and more a splinter in the thumb of the Massachusetts Colony. The citizens, once aroused, refused to drink tea so unjustly taxed; as a result the storehouses on the tea docks became so full they were in danger of bursting. The Colonists decided accordingly that incoming ships should be sent smartly home with their cargoes.

Still the ships continued to come, nor would they go. The time was ripe for action. No one knows just what went on behind the closed doors of Paul Revere's house and in the homes of certain of the other adventurous patriots. But it seems evident that for the time being the silversmith left his trade and discussed with his family the best materials for fringed breeches, and the best kind of stain for dying the skin a red brown. At any rate, one fine evening there emerged from Paul Revere's door, not a dignified gentleman in a fine gray homespun suit, well-knit hose, silver buckles on his shoes, and a warm greatcoat upon his arm; but rather an Indian brave walking softly on his leather moccasins, looking very fierce

A Silver Sugar Bowl, by Paul Revere.

although a bit portly and well fed for a red man. Other braves joined him and led a wildly enthusiastic, though orderly, group of citizens down to Griffen's Wharf, where the *Dartmouth* and two other tea ships lay at anchor.

The Indians, who, strangely enough, spoke good Colonial English, made straight for the ships; up the ladders they went like so many lithe cats. Spreading terror

A Silver Pitcher, by Paul Revere.

among the sailors and brandishing their hatchets and tomahawks, they danced their war dance. But this was by no means a celebration. The savages went down into the hold and dragged up three hundred and forty-two chests of tea. There was neither noise nor confusion. Some one must have led these red men; who it was, history does not record. But who better than Paul Revere?

As the townspeople began to understand what was happening, they made their way to the docks, carrying lanterns and torches. With intent faces, strangely

[165]

lit by the flickering light, they watched in silence eighteen thousand pounds' (about ninety thousand dollars') worth of tea go down into the salt water of Boston Harbor. So well did these strange Indians work that in three hours' time everything was over; the men were in their various homes; all was in good order. The Colonists reported that "property rights had been respected"; nothing was harmed—except the tea.

Before leaving, however, the workers turned their pockets inside out to see if any of the tea had lodged there. They would not have a leaf of it on their persons! If any one seemed to be wavering at the thought of a warm drink of that which had so long been denied him, he was searched and not too gently. One man hid just a bit in the lining of his coat, but this was found and promptly followed the contents of the chests.

When Paul Revere returned to his workbench, it was not to fashion fine tea services as had been his habit, but to make tankards for ale, mugs for milk. No tea was drunk except by renegades. The Colonial ladies had had the pleasant custom of dropping into one another's houses for a chat and a cup of comfort; often they carried their own cups and saucers and spoons with them. Such things were not owned in large quantities save by the wealthiest of the town of Boston. Now at tea time they consoled themselves as best they might with "balsamic hyperion," made from the dried leaves of the raspberry plant, or, perhaps, the dried leaves of thyme and other savory herbs. Savory, but indeed a poor substitute for the brew of which they were all so fond. But who would be a Tory in those good rebel days!

Thursday, December 13, 1773, was the day when the fishes and gulls of Boston Harbor received what was probably the surprise of their lives. The following two years were years of unwearying service on the part of Paul Revere. He was in his saddle at night more often than in his bed, carrying messages hither and yon. By spring of the year 1775 the British were getting more and more active, the Colonists more and more watchful. On the evening of April 18, those on guard in Boston noticed that the British were marching to the bottom of Boston Common. It seemed clear that they were probably going to cross over to Charlestown and from there go down to Lexington and Concord, where the Colonists' stores were kept in large quantity and where John Hancock and Samuel Adams were staying.

About ten o'clock that night Dr. Warren, Revere's friend and one of the nation's stanchest patriots, sent for him and begged that he set off to warn Hancock and Adams and to give the alarm to the Minute Men as he rode. Revere arranged for signals in the Old North Church, two if the British went by water, one if they marched by land.

Then Paul Revere went home to get ready for his ride. It probably seemed very little different to him from any other ride he had taken. Of course he was in danger of capture. But every day he had had to dodge British sentries, who would certainly have seized him had they guessed the contents of his saddle bags. In a calm, businesslike way he gathered his possessions together. "I took my boots and surtout," he tells us, "and went to the north part of town where I kept a boat; two friends rowed me across Charles River, a little to the eastward where the Somerset man-of-war lay." The *Somerset* was, of course, an English vessel. This account certainly sounds calm enough. Yet there he was right under the nose of enemy guns.

It is said that he was just ready to put his foot into the boat when he remembered that he had forgotten his spurs. His faithful dog was beside him. Paul Revere wrote a note, pinned it to the dog's collar, and pointed in the direction of home. In a few moments the intelligent beast stood nosing his master's hands, the spurs fastened to his collar. Another story tells that, while waiting for the dog, it suddenly occurred to the adventurer that he had nothing with which to muffle the sound of his oars in the rowlocks. He therefore sent one of his men to a certain house in the North End. At a signal a window was opened. A few whispered words were spoken. Paul Revere muffled his oars with a flannel petticoat that had been dropped from the open window.

Paul Revere delivered his message to Hancock and Adams, slipping by groups of Redcoats with great energy and skill. He stopped at door after door, giving the alarm. He was captured that night and escaped. The next morning, when the British did attack, they found the Yankee farmers ready for them. That was their first great surprise. That the Colonists were prepared was largely due to the swiftness and keenness of Paul Revere. But he would probably have been the most surprised man in New England if he had been told that he was "making history." He had ridden and ridden hard. But what was that? Merely his duty as the "express" of the "Sons of Liberty." No one realized during his lifetime, probably, the effect that his ride had on the future of this country. Paul Revere remained all his days merely the simple, active craftsman and mechanic that he had always been.

While the war was still raging, Paul Revere turned his hand to half a dozen things at once. If any one in Boston from John Hancock down wanted something done, he was likely to stop around at Paul Revere's house. Paul Revere became the glorified handyman of the whole town, indeed of the whole country. One of the first things needed was money with which to pay the soldiers. It was Revere who received an order to make it. The first money made in wartime was printed upon the presses of Paul Revere from copper plates engraved by his hand. In August, 1777, Paul Revere engraved the seal used by the Colony until Massachusetts became a State, when he engraved the State seal used to this day.

Money was ready for the soldiers by the time the battle of Bunker Hill was over, but not so gunpowder. Commanders knew that brave as were their men, courage counted for little without ammunition. "We want gunpowder," the people said to Paul Revere. Revere obtained a letter of introduction to the owner of a powder mill in Philadelphia. The letter did him little good. He was allowed neither to ask questions nor to take notes. His powers of observation were so keen, however, that from merely seeing the mill in operation, he was able to construct a mill of his own. This he did in Canton, Massachusetts, where there was an old abandoned mill that could be rebuilt. The work of construction was begun early in 1776 and finished in May. Then Revere took charge, and the army had its powder.

While Paul Revere was still busy with the manufacture of gunpowder, the British evacuated Boston Harbor. They tried to ruin the cannon at Fort Castle William and at other fortifications. In fact, they left them in such a state that something had to be done. Send for Revere, came the order from none other than Washington himself. The cannon were soon repaired and a new carriage invented for them. This cannon-making business became a very important industry for the versatile mechanic.

When the war was at last over, Paul Revere in no way curtailed his activities. Among other things he made the engravings for a hymn book and printed it. He made medals and seals of every description. The seal of Phillips Academy, Andover, was made by him. He recalled his early skill at whittling and now and then in his leisure moments—few they must have been—he carved picture frames for the paintings made by his friend John Singleton Copley, a well-known artist of his day. At the age of fifty-one, carrying his years jauntily, he set up a store. He called it a hardware store. But it seems to have contained much more than what we of to-day call hardware. Paul Revere kept hosiery, coatings, and merchandise, "gold necklaces, lockets, rings, bracelets, beads, buttons, medals, and cases for pictures," with everything in silver that could be thought of. He often said that while he did an endless number of things, it was his business of silversmithing that was his chief means of support. Sometimes he received strange orders. Mr. Andrew Oliver wished to make a sugar dish out of an ostrich egg, and the estate of Doc. Josh. Clark, Esq. ordered "eleven Death's Head gold Rings." A bill which he made out to Mr. Samuel Adams will give some idea of the variety of his stock:

```
1785
Dec. 31    To 1-2 doz Sley bells ........................... 7.6
1786       To 1 Door lock ................................. 5
May  6     To 4 Pair hinges .............................. 5.4
           To 2 thumb catches ............................ 1.4
           To 1 brandy cock .............................. 1.9
Dec. 13    To 3 truck Bells .............................. 6
     29    To 3 sley Bells ............................... 5
1787
Jan. 10    To 1 Truck Bell ............................... 2
                                                          _____
                                                          1.13.11
              Cr.
Dec. 21    By his account settled Nov. 28, 1787 .......... 1.13.11
                                                          _____
```

Courtesy of the Museum of Fine Arts, Boston.

A Silver Teapot, by Paul Revere.

About the same time he started an iron, brass, and copper foundry; and this led to the casting of bells. One of the most famous of these is the bell which still hangs in King's Chapel, Boston. It is one of some sixty church bells cast by Paul Revere. The bells used to be tested in the foundry yard, which was usually thronged with small boys, fascinated by the clang and clamor. Sometimes they would get too near. "Look out for the mallets, boys," Paul Revere would warn them, "or your heads will ring louder than the bells."

Interesting as was this part of the foundry work, it was by no means the most important. Paul Revere now established a mill for rolling copper into flat sheets; it was the first in this country. The sheets of copper were used, among other things, on vessels to protect them from barnacles and the general wear and tear of many voyages. One of the vessels to be so equipped was the good ship *Constitution*, made so famous by young Oliver Wendell Holmes's poem, "Old Ironsides." Old Ironsides was re-coppered by Paul Revere's foundry in the year 1803. While Revere was working in his mill, a young inventor was working on a strange invention, that of the steamboat. No one thought anything would come of it. But strangely enough, Fulton was able to make his boats travel without sails and against adverse winds. It was Paul Revere who furnished two copper boilers to Messrs. Livingston and Fulton to be used on the Hudson River and New York ferry boats.

All this time Paul Revere did not forget his silver. Almost to his last days he sat at his bench, making porringers, strainers, cups, and cans. Handyman he was, handyman and great artist. Faithfully he carried on the great tradition of his craft, brought from Europe by his French father, Apollon, a tradition purified and simplified on these austere shores. At no time since has America had silver so beautiful as that made by the Colonial silversmiths. Of all these, none was more skillful than Master Paul Revere.

A Wood-carver Of Today
I. Kirchmayer

Courtesy of Mr. Kirchmayer.

The Visit of the Three Kings, by I. Kirchmayer.

A WOOD-CARVER OF TO-DAY

"Give me that slate and let me try; I can draw a dog. See if I can't." A small four-year-old stretched out his hand for the slate and pencil. With sure, competent strokes he did draw a dog. The dog was swimming. The boy had seen it only yesterday in the Ammer River, that flows through the town of Oberammergau, where he lived. In the drawing, just the dog's head appeared in the swift current and one strong paw.

"That is not such a bad-looking dog either." His brother held the slate out at arm's length and eyed it critically.

"Didn't I say I could?" asked the little boy triumphantly.

So began the long years of work that went into the making of a wood-carver of to-day, a certain I. Kirchmayer. He did not stop with the drawing of the dog. He went on and on; he drew all sorts of animals, especially horses. "I drew horses," says Mr. Kirchmayer, "because I was always a little afraid of them; they fascinated me. Perhaps I thought I was bigger than the horse if I could draw him. Cows and even oxen I was quite at home with. When I was only three, I used to ride them to the pasture. But a horse now, galloping and kicking. That is a different matter when you are only three, or even four."

Drawing was fun; but when he was six, this small person found something even better. He found a bit of soft wood and a knife. He guessed he'd whittle. Looking out through the open window, he saw a flock of sheep on their hilly pasture with young lambs gamboling about. He guessed he'd make a lamb. He did. It was a pretty good lamb. It was almost as good as the ones his father made. At least the little boy thought so. His father was something of a carver; he made animals and crucifixes which he sold to tourists in the village.

The young Kirchmayer carved a great many lambs. He was sitting on the doorstep on a certain sunny morning when one of his friends came by.

"Will you give me that lamb?" asked his companion.

"No," said the youthful carver positively. "No, I won't give it to you; but I will sell it to you." That is what his father did. Why not he?

"How much will you sell it for?"

"One penny."

His future purchaser put a grimy fist reluctantly into his pocket and drew out his last coin.

"Give me the lamb," he said and walked quickly away.

That was easy. Then and there the little Kirchmayer decided on his profession. Nothing could be simpler. You made a lamb; you sold it for a penny. You bought cakes and sweets. You were rich. What a world, what a very fine world indeed! But, as often happens with such rosy plans, things did not work out quite according to the scheme. "I had a hard time collecting," Mr. Kirchmayer will tell you with a smile, "but I always managed to do it."

"Look here," he would say some fine day when he was almost seven, "look here, you owe me two cents."

"No such thing."

Quickly the carver would dive into his friend's pocket and bring out two lambs. "You give me two cents, or I'll take 'em home and sell 'em to Hans."

"You give me back my two lambs."

"They aren't your lambs; they're mine. I made them, and you haven't paid for them."

"Well . . . well . . . I was just going to. What are you in such a hurry about?"

"If you were just going to, do it."

"I haven't got two cents."

"Then you haven't got two lambs either." The carver walked off, the lambs in his pocket. That same afternoon his friend came to call.

"You give me back my two lambs."

"You give me two cents."

Again most reluctantly a fist would go into a pocket, and the money would lie in the eager palm of the carver; the lambs were returned. But how he had worked. Collecting was not so simple. Carving was easier.

[173]

Courtesy of Mr. Kirchmayer.

The Virgin Mary,
by I. Kirchmayer.

One day his kinsman, George Lang, who was a professional carver and had orders from Munich, from Augsburg, and even from Berlin, came to visit the Kirchmayer family. As usual the young whittler was at work. He had deserted his lambs and was making a cow, his first cow. The uncle took the cow in his hand. He looked at it; then he looked at the little Kirchmayer. "You will be a carver like me some day," he said, "like me only more than me. See that you work hard. Not too much carving without drawing. Drawing will help your carving. Carve and carve, but draw more."

The little boy promised that he would learn to draw; and that fall when he started to public school, he asked permission to add an extra drawing lesson each week to the two lessons provided in the regular program. Then he took two more lessons at the evening school. This made five lessons a week. He had certain kinsmen among the Langs who were potters. They taught him of their art, too. He early learned the feel of the clay in his fingers and got a sense of how bowls and vases build up either in coils or spin magically upon the potter's wheel. Sometimes after a lesson he would model animals from clay. This was fun, but somehow the knife fitted more naturally to his hand. It was carving that he liked best. But he did not forget the drawing.

All the while he was receiving instruction in school, he was receiving even more from just living in the place where he happened to have been born. Oberammergau, in the Bavarian Alps, has a life all its own, quite unlike anything else in the world. The activities of the entire town are centered around the Passion Play, which has been given once in every ten years since the sixteen hundreds, with one exception, the performance after the World War, which was deferred until 1922. The

[174]

play tells the story of the last days of the life of Christ; it includes tableaux of various Old Testament scenes which foreshadowed the great events of the New Testament.

The Passion Play is the direct descendant of the old miracle and morality plays given during the Middle Ages. These were often performed in the church. The Passion Play, however, was acted before such crowds that it was first of all given in the graveyard. Now it has a great theater all its own. But plays and tableaux are still given in the church at Oberammergau on feast days and at Christmas and Easter. The Passion Play attracts tourists literally from all over the world. They come, thousands of them, to see the performance given by these simple Bavarian peasants. The funds gained from the Play are divided into four parts: the first goes to the poor; the second to the expenses of the theater; the third to the art school, the hospital, and all other useful institutions of the village; the fourth part to the small salaries of the actors. If any is left over, it is divided among the inhabitants of the village.

Seven hundred people are needed in the Play. Those villagers who have no actual part are many of them busy at costumes, at stage settings, or stage properties. The actors consider it the greatest possible honor to be in the Play. The man who takes the part of *Christus* is of course the greatest of them all. He is treated by every one with the utmost respect. The Langs, kinsmen of the young Kirchmayer, gave one *Christus* to the Play, the great Anton Lang. And the young carver himself was in the cast. When he was about twelve years old, he was given the part of Joseph "with the pretty coat," the coat of many colors. Being one of the cast does not mean simply being a good actor. It means being a fine, upstanding person throughout all the years when the play is in preparation.

All Oberammergau thinks of the great Passion

Courtesy of Mr. Kirchmayer.
Motherhood,
by I. Kirchmayer.

[175]

Play as one of the things for which it lives. The industries of the town are all touched by it. There are many carvers. These usually work upon the religious subjects which the Play suggests. The walls of the houses are painted with figures of the Virgin, of St. John, of David the shepherd boy. Even the potters model religious figures. Everywhere the old stories live as if they were taking place to-day. Indeed, they do take place whenever the Passion Play is given. The little Kirchmayer and his friends knew their saints and their Bible characters as well as they knew one another.

These Bible characters were not merely people in a book, but living, breathing folk clothed in brilliant colors and speaking in German. They knew their fellow citizens not only as Hans, as Frank, as Wilhelm, but also by their Passion Play names: Joseph, Pilate, John the Beloved Disciple. Often in their own way the children acted out the story of Daniel accused before King Darius, the Israelites bitten by fiery serpents, or Jonah and the whale. The little Kirchmayer took especial delight in being a fiery serpent. The crawling about was a trifle hard on his clothes, however. When these children grew a little older, it seemed as natural as breathing for them to take parts on the stage. In fact, many of them actually did appear almost as soon as they could walk. They were young angels or children in the scene which shows the Israelites gathering manna fallen from Heaven.

All of this was as real to them as the great mountain-peak, Kofel, that overlooks the whole village, and as the iron cross which marks its summit, the first thing you see in the morning, all burning gold with the sun, the last thing you see at night, silvery in the moonlight. The Ettalerberg, standing massive against the noonday sky, was not more clear to their sight than was the Mount of Olives. And as for miracles, they happened everywhere. Was not their own old monastery of Ettal built because of one?

The children knew well that long ago, after the German Emperor, Ludwig the Bavarian, had been crowned in Rome, he was basely attacked in the city of Milan. At the monastery of St. Victor he prayed for aid. A monk appeared before him, bearing a beautiful image of the Blessed Virgin. The holy man promised help to the Emperor if, on arriving in the valley of the Ammer, he would found a Benedictine monastery and place the lovely image there. Ludwig gave his oath; and as he rode up the Ettalerberg, his horse fell three times on his knees and could go no farther. The Emperor took it as a sign and, dismounting, ordered a little chapel to be hastily constructed where he could place the image until he could lay the foundation stone of the great monastery; this he did in the year 1330. And does it not stand there still, even though its monastic days are past and it has become the home of a great count!

These things, as natural to the little Kirchmayer as the fact that rabbits hop, roosters crow, boys whistle, and crows caw, were perhaps the most important part of his training as a carver of saints. These early impressions going through his mind, gorgeous pageants in gold and blue, in scarlet and russet; men, women, children, prophets, queens, angels with beating wings, were all to appear one day in the form of figures carved in oak, cherry, or pear-wood.

As for school itself, he persevered well enough; but his chief interest was always the drawing. He did so well in this that when he was fourteen the authorities came visiting his parents. They had decided, they said, to give industrious Master Kirchmayer a scholarship in the drawing school. So splendidly did he progress that he earned another at Partenkirchen, a town in the mountains not far from Oberammergau. Those were good days, and he worked hard. Better still were to come.

To his great delight he next earned a traveling scholarship. Now he would see what lay beyond his native hills. First he went to Augsburg. There he studied what is known as anatomy; that is, the construction of the human body. He learned to know its bones and muscles and tendons. He soon realized that because of its form the human arm can make only certain movements, take only certain positions. Realizing this, he could not go very far wrong in the drawing of an arm. The same thing is true for all parts of the body.

From Augsburg he went to Munich. Here he worked evenings and drew by day. It was a busy life, but there was time now and then on Sundays and holidays for walks with his fellow students; and always there were museums, where he was constantly studying the work of great masters. Museums were to these young artists what the laboratories are to young scientists. Here they found the material from which they could see how art has grown and how others have understood it. From Munich he went to Paris. Here also was more studying and more drawing, always drawing. If there were times when he had to pull his belt a bit tight so as not to notice how hungry he was, well, what was that when it is spring in Paris and you are young! Following Paris, came London, where he remained for two years. More work, more drawing, more studying of great painters and sculptors.

He was quite a man now, about eighteen. He must set about earning his living. You can't depend upon scholarships forever. He turned his steps back to his mountains, back to George Lang, who was a professional carver. With his kinsman as teacher, he began to work as a professional himself. He learned not only to think of

Heavenly Music, by I. Kirchmayer.

what he had in hand, but to think of it in relation to its setting, the place it was to go. The art of the carver is usually very closely related to the art of the architect, the designer of buildings.

A carver must make his work show for what it is, but at the same time it must always remain a part of the architect's plan. It must never obtrude or overshadow; neither must it be small or insignificant. There is a nice question of balance here; with his greater experience George Lang was able to help. The figures that young Kirchmayer carved were in what is known as the Gothic tradition, the tradition of the wood-carvers of the thirteenth, fourteenth, and fifteenth centuries. These early men thought of themselves not merely as carvers of single figures but as workers who were adding their part to the whole beauty of church, monastery, or castle.

Though the figures created by the young carver carried on the Gothic idea, yet they were by no means copies. They were a part of the world in which young Kirchmayer was growing up. The faces had a more personal expression in them than had the faces carved in the Middle Ages; they were more like portraits. There was more variety in the poses of the figures, more freedom of movement. They were new, even though they had in them many of the old ideas. One thing which the medieval world taught the eager artist and from which he never departed was the treatment of costume. It is always simple, always what is known as conventionalized; that is to say, treated according to an artistic plan rather than as an imitation of nature.

Look, for instance, at the drapery on the Madonna in "Christmas in Heaven." The lines are lovely, soft, and flowing; but in a real robe you would have much more detail; you would see the fastenings, the linings, all the tiny folds and wrinkles. These, says Mr. Kirchmayer, have no place in sculpture. It is beauty of surface and line that you want, not hooks and eyes. Here he and the great Gothic carvers are equally wise.

In the studio of George Lang, Mr. Kirchmayer was laying the foundation for all his future work. Life was kind enough to him there in the little Bavarian village. But the great world called; he was once more anxious for adventure. He, too, set sail. When he was but twenty, he arrived in New York, alone. Mr. Kirchmayer will tell you that it was a time of carving and starving, of coffee and rolls and very little else. The starving, fortunately, did not last long. He became connected with the firm of A. Kimbel and Sons in New York. You could not keep so good a workman down. With great rapidity he went up through the ranks until he became foreman.

After Kimbel and Sons came the Herter Brothers in Boston, where he was also foreman. He took charge of the plant, but always he was at work upon his own blocks of mahogany, cherry, or oak. He never for one single second ceased to be an artist working for the love of his job. When he first arrived in America, there was little employment for a carver save in houses. He toiled over mantels, stairways, wainscots, and even furniture now and then. He says he carved his way from cover to cover in Jones's "Grammar of Ornament," a kind of dictionary of different styles

Courtesy of Mr. Kirchmayer.

Saint Anthony of Padua,
by I. Kirchmayer.

[179]

of decoration from every age and country. Though this work added not a little to his natural skill and knowledge, he had not yet come into his own. But soon there came a change; America began to build some of her largest churches. They could not be built without Mr. Kirchmayer!

Now he had come home; now he was again in the world of the Passion Play with its pageants of glowing figures. He carved them for such great architects as Vaughn, Cram, Richardson, Goodhue, Corbusier. All over this country, church altars, church screens, panels, figures large and small, began to appear. These were what Mr. Kirchmayer calls "American Gothic," a new term in art. By it he meant the blending of the New World with the Old.

What had the machine to do with all this? Had it any place? "Yes," says Mr. Kirchmayer, "use it, but do not abuse it." There are certain things a machine can do as well as a man; as for instance long moldings where the same pattern is repeated again and again. Let the machine do it and be thankful for long hours of labor saved. But let it stop when it can no longer help. Single figures, groups of figures: here the machine is of no use. It only does harm. Here only the hand of the master carver can serve.

Six years ago Mr. Kirchmayer retired from his position. He works now entirely as an independent artist; he is enjoying a well-earned peace. One of his most recent figures is called "Motherhood." The little angel heads clustering in her crown, nestling on her shoulder, held in her slender hands, are the children. "All children are angels," says Mr. Kirchmayer, "until we spoil them." There is a good deal of wisdom in that sentence if you think about it long enough. A figure near that of "Motherhood" is one of Mr. Kirchmayer's many representations of the Madonna. Here she seems not so much the Mother of the Child whom she holds; but rather she is the reigning Queen of Heaven and of the Church. She is above all dignified and regal. Bishops and princes would kneel before her. The Child is not so much a child as a little king before whom half the world bows in reverence. How straight He holds himself in His Mother's arms as if to receive the worship of His people!

All of these figures come naturally to the hand of Mr. Kirchmayer. Did he not see such groups presented before his wondering childish gaze, in all their glory of movement and color? He has but to remember the tableaux and the scenes of the little Bavarian village. With his inner eye he can see the blaze of color: purples, reds, golds, blues, and greens; he can see the meaningful gestures; he can hear again the songs of the choristers. All this goes into his carving.

Christmas in Heaven, by I. Kirchmayer.

Take, for instance, "Christmas in Heaven." Who but a man so trained and so brought up could have planned it?—the Madonna suspended in the wreath made up of little angel heads; the angels with their hymns of praise; even the ox there among the clouds as he was once humbly kneeling in the hay at Bethlehem. The Madonna is here the simple Mary, mother of the Child Jesus. She holds Him out to a waiting world made up of simple folk. He opens his arms wide as though in acknowledgment of the welcome given Him by the centuries.

Below Him, deep in their books, are the bishops and fathers of the church. If only they would look up! Below also are the saints: St. Paul with the sword,

Courtesy of Mr. Kirchmayer.

Panels for St. Paul's Church, Chicago, by I. Kirchmayer.

St. John with the cup, St. Stephen with the book, and the great and terrible St. Ambrose, grasping the handle of the scourge. They, too, despite all their wisdom, fail to lift their eyes. They do not know that at dawn on Christmas morning, Jesus becomes for a few moments the Child that He may thus simply reënter the hearts of men.

The panel from St. Paul's Church is made up of scenes in the lives of four great men. On the right in the upper panel is Amos, the herdsman of Tekoa, who was given the gift of prophecy. Sitting among his flocks, he foretold the punishments coming to the wayward Israelites and to the Oriental cities of Tyre and

Sidon. Below is Samuel, the great ruler and anointer of kings, who put both Saul and David on the throne. Looking through the door of the temple, he sees in a blinding light the face of God.

On the left, in the upper panel, is St. Peter; the keys of heaven and hell are in his hands; he receives the spirit of his Master. In the panels below, St. Stephen, cross in hand, is being tried for his beliefs. His words led to his martyrdom; he was stoned for his faith.

"The Angel" is one of the musicians of heaven. Bending above his violin, he plays wondrous sweet strains. Sometimes through the half-opened gates of Paradise they float down to earth. A man looks up and dreams; a child begins to laugh; some one who had never tried before, writes a poem; a farmer plants a field for the joy of turning up the long black furrows. "St. Anthony of Padua" in his monk's robe stands with the Child in his arms. St. Anthony was one of the most beloved followers of the good St. Francis of Assisi. Like St. Francis he was full of pity for the poor and wretched, full of joy in the world with its tall hills and ever-winding roads. So great was his faith that once, for a moment, he felt the Child there in his own strong hands.

"The Visit of the Three Kings" shows how Mr. Kirchmayer fits his decoration into the plan of the architect. His figures are perfectly clear, but they are obviously a part of a great whole. To the right are three who have heard the angels tell that a King is born but who will not stir. It is a myth, a story; though angels sing it, they will not believe. To the left are the Three Kings, who believed so surely that, guided by holy messengers, they traveled across unending desert sands to find Him who was born in a stable. The center panel shows Mary, Joseph, and the Child, little guessing that they are about to receive gifts of gold, frankincense, and myrrh. It is the heading of this chapter.

Last of all is the crib, carved for some fortunate child who will sleep in a bed guarded always by four angels made by a master's hand.

Ask Mr. Kirchmayer: "How do you carve a figure?" Quite clearly and simply he will tell you: "First of all I plan what I am to make. If it is a saint I am to carve, I read the history of that saint until I know just what kind of man he was. On my block in charcoal I draw the figure—always nude. Then in crayon I draw the drapery over the figure. Then I chop it out." "Chop it out" is an artist's phrase. It hardly describes the delicate workmanship such as you see, say on the moldings of the crib or on the wings of the angels. You will remember that when he was very young, Mr. Kirchmayer learned that "drawing is the bones of

Courtesy of Mr. Kirchmayer.

Crib Designed by Ralph Adams Cram, Carved by I. Kirchmayer.

carving." First of all he draws. He draws the figure in the nude because he learned to think that way in Augsburg, where he studied anatomy. By drawing it so, he cannot get lost in the drapery and make an arm too long from shoulder to elbow, a leg too short from knee to ankle. Having assured himself that the proportions—the relations of one part to another—are right, then he can put on the clothes, cover the figure with drapery. And at last he is ready to carve, to begin.

To-day Mr. Kirchmayer lives in East Cambridge, "the Bowery of Cambridge," he calls it. "It is better for me," he says. "If I had a studio in Boston in the Back Bay, people would soon begin to complain of the noise I make and I should have to move. But in the Bowery nobody cares; I can work in my own kitchen." It is rather a rough place, he will tell you. Most of his neighbors are foreigners who have not lived in this country very long. They are suspicious of strangers and are apt to be quarrelsome and even dangerous to newcomers. "But it is all right for me," says Mr. Kirchmayer with a smile. "I can come and go as I like; they are my friends; they would never harm me. That is because they know I am a carver of saints."

So let the reader leave this hardy carver of saints, who with all jollity and good will is carrying on the old tradition here in the world of to-day, adding to it much that is his own. "The great days for art in this country are but beginning," he prophesies with a smile; "we are only now awakening."

MASTERSMITH
FRANK KORALEWSKY

MASTER SMITH

About fifty years ago on the shores of the Baltic Sea, in northern Germany, a small boy, blue-eyed, round, and very vigorous, was growing up. His head was full of stories and of old folk tales. Wherever the children gathered together to hear some good granny tell of Snow White, of Red Riding Hood, of the gnomes that live under the earth, of the hidden gold of the Daughters of the Rhine, or of the great deeds of the hero Siegfried, the little boy was always sure to be among them, big-eyed and listening.

He used also to watch his neighbors at their work: the carpenter, who planed off long shavings coiled like golden springs; the mason, who laid stones one on top of another, firm and straight and strong, building a wall. He saw fishermen start out in their boats, praying for a good day's catch. He followed the farmer at his plowing and seeding. All these things were good. But when he grew up, there was something else he wanted to do.

Hours at a time he would stand in the door of the forge of the master smith of the town, half hypnotized by the hungry flames on the anvil and by the iron, once so hard and black, now red and pliant under the master's hammer. The anvil seemed to him like an altar to the old god, Loki, god of fire; and the iron, sputtering and sparking, seemed to him like some spirit chained and enchanted by that god. How he longed to be like Loki and like the master smith. Yes, that is what he would be when he grew up.

There were many men in the shop. Some were hammering out heavy bars for a gate; others were working upon leaves as delicate as if they had grown on a newly budded tree—these for a screen in front of a church altar. Some were burnishing and polishing, and still others were bent over the intricate parts of a great lock to be put on the Burgomaster's new house. It had to be both heavy and strong. Was not the Burgomaster the richest man in all the town?

Some day he would make a lock like that. Yes, he would! He stood until the afternoon shadows deepened, until the pines upon the hillsides were black, and the great sea was like a still silver plate. "Frank, Frank Koralewsky," some one would call. "It is supper time. Come right home. What are you thinking of?" What was he thinking of, indeed? Always of the licking flames and the angrily protesting iron, of the miners, almost as black as the dwarfs themselves, who dug the treasures for the master smith. How angry the dwarfs were to have their precious iron ore taken from them!

The little boy nodded over his bowl of porridge; and when he went to bed, he dreamed that he was climbing a high mountain. When he reached the top, he heard a raven complaining and cawing, flapping its wings in anger and distress. The cause of its displeasure was a tiny man not half so tall as the little boy himself. He was dressed in dusty brown; he wore a tall peaked hat and had a beard so long that it almost touched his knees. The wee fellow bent his back over a heavy fork. He was trying to move a great bowlder. The more he tugged, the more furiously the raven cawed.

Suddenly the little man heaved the bowlder high into the air; the mountain rumbled; the raven flew into a tall tree. Then slowly, quietly, the mountain opened. Down, down at the foot of a dark crevice there was a bright gleam as though a star had fallen in. With a chuckle, the little man began to climb down. The raven flew at him and tried to pick out his eyes; but the little man only laughed a dry, dusty laugh and clambered down and down. With a terrible cry, the raven flew away.

"The gnome's found the bird's secret," the little boy whispered in his dream. The little boy followed the dwarf and looked over the precipice. The treasure was so bright it almost blinded him: diamonds, pearls, gold, emeralds as green as spring, and rubies like Loki's fire. "Oh," cried the little boy, "Oh. . . ." Then he awoke. The moon was looking straight into his eyes.

The next day, bright and early, he ran off to the hills to see if he could find the raven's rock; but all he got was some bruises, a few berries, and a rent in his new blouse. When he returned from his journey, he stopped once more to watch the master smith. He soon forgot his disappointment of the morning and the torn suit as he watched the sparks fly and listened to the clink, clank, clink, clonk of the hammers on the anvils. It was summer time. He could look as long as he liked.

The following winter it was different. Some one caught him by the coat-tail as he was running off to the forge one day, put the little boy's hand in his older brother's, and said, "Now you are going to school; now you will learn to read and write." "Read and write," thought the little boy. "Poof, what is that? Any one can learn that. Only the smith can hammer." But he did go to school; he did learn to read and write. He learned to do long sums, so long that for a while they chased all the dreams out of his head and all the stories. He quite forgot the gnomes.

When he was fourteen, his father said: "Now it is time you learned a trade. What shall it be?" In spite of the fact that he was now so big, the boy's heart almost stopped beating. "Oh, I don't know," he said; "perhaps I'll be a clock-maker, or perhaps I'll work in the counting house, or maybe I'd like to be a smith, a master smith, though I have heard that it is very hard and dirty work."

"Well," said his father, "a man cannot earn his living by washing his hands under the pump all day. You could not have a better master than the one here in our town."

"But," said the boy, "perhaps I'd better be a builder. People must always have houses, you know."

"Well, a man must have a lock for his house, too, and a lanthorn for a light. The church must have grilles and gates."

"I might be the captain of a fishing fleet."

"A long and dangerous time you'd have before you were ever a captain."

"There's Hans, who is going to be a student and a professor."

"A fine student you'd be, a boy who does not love his Latin!"

"Well then, if you say so, I'll be a dirty smith." And the boy walked out of the room with a scowl on his brow and his heart bursting with happiness. It would never do to show it, he, a man of fourteen.

The next morning he was duly apprenticed to the master smith just as boys were apprenticed back in the days of the early guilds of armorers, wood-carvers, tapestry-weavers, or dyers of cloth. For three years he would have to work in the shop, serving here, serving there, before he could become a journeyman and go his way, a free worker. In the beginning he had to wait on the other men in the shop, go where he was called. "Here, boy, hand me that bar of iron." . . . "More wood on the fire, there!" . . . "Be quick with the bellows" . . . "*Dummkopf*, can't you hold that steady while I hammer?" So many commands, his head spun. This was work and plenty of it. No time for dreams now; but had he known it, the young apprentice with a smudge on his nose and his blue eyes snapping like sparks did not look very different from the friends of his babyhood, the wee men, the gnomes.

He soon discovered, mostly by watching, that the work of the master smith covered two distinct branches of the craft: that of the blacksmith and that of what

The Forging of a Candelabra, by Frank Koralewsky.

The Forging of a Candelabra, by Frank Koralewsky.

The Forging of a Candelabra, by Frank Koralewsky.

we may call the locksmith. The blacksmith worked his iron only when hot; his tools were hammer, anvil, and bellows. The work that he turned out was on the whole rather heavy in its construction. He made such things as great hinges for doors, heavy grilles, iron-bound chests, andirons, and cranes. The locksmith worked his iron when cold; his tools were more like those of a jeweler: saw, chisel, file, punch, and gouge. The locksmith made, of course, locks, finely decorated; he made clocks, weather vanes, and more delicate hinges and grilles. These were often cut from sheet iron and were sometimes as finely interlaced as a growing plant. Both the branches of the craft had to be learned by the young apprentice.

From the talk of the men around him, he gathered something of the history of iron. He heard that it had been used in the lands of the Far East as much as fifteen hundred years before it was generally employed in Western Europe. The Greeks knew iron and with it smashed through countless battle fronts. They did not use it so widely in other ways as did the Romans. With the Romans iron was almost as common—in their households, at least—as it is with us.

When the Romans went with Caesar to conquer Gaul and Britain, they found the barbarians, as they called the inhabitants of those countries, all ready to meet them with iron weapons. Though the making of objects of iron was a comparatively new art with the Northerners, yet all the Gauls were very skillful and especially the Belgæ, a Germanic tribe living in the northern part of Gaul. After the time of Cæsar's conquest there seems to have been much more travel in Western Europe than there had been before; perhaps this was due somewhat to the fine Roman roads. As a result of much going about, the knowledge of working in iron spread very rapidly.

Throughout the thirteenth century—the twelve hundreds—the workers in iron were mostly blacksmiths, handling their metal hot and turning out objects which on the whole were rather massive. Then came about a hundred years of change or transition in which the blacksmith was finding out the ways of the locksmith, learning to handle his metal while cold. In the fourteen and fifteen hundreds the delicate work of the locksmith held its greatest sway.

The master smith, under whom the young apprentice labored, had the benefit of all the knowledge gained from these many hundreds of years. He had also much of the knowledge of the modern world. He knew, of course, all about heating iron until it is liquid and then casting it in a mold. But this he considered the work of machines, not men. He limited his craft to the making of those things which could best be wrought by a tool in the human hand.

After a time the boy was given his first piece of iron to hammer into a long
flat bar for a gate. He began to know the strength of his own arm as well as its
ache and weakness; he began to get used to the feel of the metal under his hammer. Hard and unyielding as it seemed when cold, it had surprising qualities
when heated or even when hammered cold. Too many strokes in one place and
the iron spread and thinned like taffy; the bar became more like a pancake than

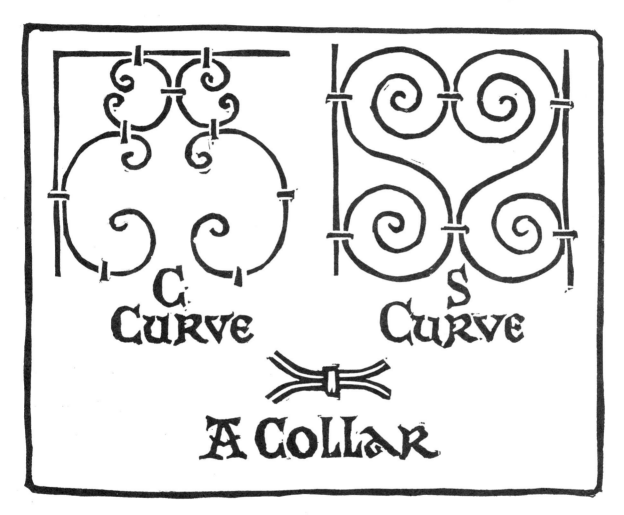

a bar. But as time went on, the lad was able to foresee this; he learned when to
hit and when not to.

He was allowed more and more to take part in the various processes of the
work. He learned how to flatten out the end of a bar, split it into the form of two
leaves, or make a fleur-de-lis form or a thistle. He labored hard until he could
make a good C curve. Having learned this, he found out how to fasten his C curves

together with a wisp of iron called a collar and so make all sorts of charming patterns. Finally, he began to *weld* two pieces of iron together. It was not so easy. The first time, he heated the iron too hot, and it crumbled under his hammer; the next time he did not heat it hot enough, and the two pieces would not stay together. Oh, there was more than one trick to this trade.

He helped the journeymen polish and burnish, and after a while he had his first bouts at working in the cold metal with chisel and saw. This was a new world altogether. Very little that he had learned in the blacksmithing branch of his trade helped him now. A delicate touch was needed instead of the steady swing of the hammer. All that he knew of drawing—he was studying that constantly—had to be called to his aid. In the chiseling of an animal's head, say on the end of a poker, he had to turn sculptor. In engraving a vine-like design on the ring of a door-knocker he had almost to turn jeweler. Would there ever be an end to things he had to know, he wondered.

It was not long before the master smith began to notice the boy. "That lad is a likely fellow," he said. "He has the craft in his fingers. He will learn." And learn he did. No one said very much, but the men gave him a chance to watch and try. You cannot tell a craftsman the strength of his material; you cannot tell him when to make this blow and when to refrain from making that. Nothing can tell him but trying and trying again. The boy learned without many lessons; he learned by sad mistakes and bitter experiences, but he learned. He gained not only by doing but by looking. If ever there was a moment when he was not being called this way or that, he stood and gazed over the shoulders of the journeymen. They were kind about his eager, intelligent questions.

The months went by; and as they passed, the boy grew taller and stronger. Great strength and quickness came into his hands. And his head was full of plans. He would make this and that—as soon as they would let him. Sometimes early in the morning he would be at the anvil working on something of his own, perhaps a cock for a weather vane on the barn. When it was finished, his sister said it looked more like a pig; but that's the way sisters are sometimes. You cannot attach too much importance to what they say. At twilight after the day's work was over, he would beg for permission to linger on at the forge. All his thought was on his work. No place for dreams now or for tales.

Before he or any one else knew it, his three years had passed. He was soon to be tested to see if he was skillful enough to become a free journeyman. To prove his ability he had to make something all his own. This was to be judged by his mas-

An Italian Garden Gate, by Frank Koralewsky.
The Crane Estate, Ipswich, Massachusetts.

ter and other competent men. If it came up to the standard, he could go his way; if not—well, he had failed. First of all, he had to decide what he would undertake. He chose a lock. Then he had to make his drawing or design and submit it to the judges. If they approved, he had to determine how long it would take him to make the lock. If he finished it much too soon, this would count against him; it would show that he could not estimate time correctly. If he was not through when the time was up, then his work would not be finished. That would indeed be a disaster. Next he had to figure out how much material the lock would take. The required number of bars of iron were given to him. Each one was stamped. He had to use his metal in such a way that the stamps would all show in the finished piece. This was to prove that he had used all that was given him and no more. If much was left over, that was bad; if he did not have all that he needed, that was worse. His precious lock would be only partly done. There were so many "ifs" to the whole affair. His task was a very anxious one.

He made his design for the lock. To his abounding joy, it was accepted. Then for many months, quite separated from his companions, the boy worked alone. Now and then one of the judges would enter the room and stand over the lad, shaking a gray head wisely. Cold shivers ran down the young apprentice's spine. What if he should fail, what if he should take too long, or have too little metal? The clever fingers flew. He worked on the metal, now heating it, now letting it cool. It followed the demands of his hammer or chisel, shaping itself to his will. Now, indeed, he was a god; now the iron was his slave. The dream he had had as a little boy was coming true. But he had no time to think of that.

At home he hardly spoke, so full of his task was he; and he quite forgot his friends and the sports they had together in the forest or beside the sea. His very sleep was filled with the sound of the hammer on the anvil. And he would start up in the middle of the night wondering if he had done this or failed to do that. The weeks flew by. Time was eating his great chance in hungry mouthfuls. It began to seem like a race. But he would not hurry.

Slowly, carefully he worked on to the very end. And at last on the appointed day, the lock was done. All the stamps on the bars of iron could be plainly seen. He had chosen enough material, but not too much. The judges came and examined his lock; it was good to look upon, sound, and cleverly made in its mechanical parts. "Yes, that boy will do." They made him a free journeyman like themselves. He was his own master. He could come and go as he liked. He was a man!

Within a very short time he gathered his few possessions together and started upon his year of travel, his *wanderjahr*. He went throughout Germany, working here and there, and at each place proving himself a laborer worthy of his hire. Many a good master wanted to keep the young man. But no, he would not stay. He was out to see the world as young men have been since the world began. He thought, too, of lands beyond the sea, of America. And one day, having said farewell to his home, to his family and friends, he actually set sail. He landed in

Andirons, by Frank Koralewsky.

the city of Boston, where he was fortunate enough to meet a man who, like himself, had learned his craft in Germany, knew it well, and loved it. The young journeyman started to work with Mr. Krasser of the Krasser Iron Company of Boston. There he remained; and for several years, since the death of Mr. Krasser, he has himself been manager of the plant.

In the shop the men work much as they worked when Frank Koralewsky was learning his trade in Straalsund by the Baltic Sea. There are no machines. All the work is done by hand, whether it be the delicate part of a lock or the great supports of a spiral stairway. As you walk about, it is hard to believe that you are in America. There is so much of the Old World there, the old respect for the craft and for the power of the human hand. Besides all the labor of managing the company, Mr. Koralewsky has found time to keep on with his own work. And strangely enough, here in America, far from the woods and the sea of his native country, the dwarfs and the gnomes have come back to him.

Courtesy of Mr. Koralewsky.

Jewel Box, by Frank Koralewsky.

The jewel box, which is illustrated, is the dream that he had as a little boy. There is the mountain; there, the raven in the tree; there, the dwarf bending over his fork, prying away at a heavy stone. If you want to get at what is hidden, you touch a certain branch on the tree at the right. This loosens the stone. Then you push it aside; press down on the trunk of the tree also at the right, and

Courtesy of Mr. Koralewsky.

A Detail of a Jewel Box, by Frank Koralewsky.

behold, the mountain opens as if by magic and inside is a jewel box, lined with soft velvet for your treasure!

The lock, also illustrated, won for Mr. Koralewsky the prize at the Panama-Pacific Exposition. Did he not say as a little child that he would some day make a wonderful lock? Upon it he has put the story of "Snow White and the Seven

Dwarfs." While he was a young journeyman, he was too busy for such things as fairy tales; but as he bent over his work at the forge in Boston, they all came trooping round the grown man that he had become. He remembered perfectly how:

Once upon a time there lived a wicked Queen. She had in her care a very beautiful young girl whose hair was black, whose eyes were dark and sparkling, whose skin was so fair that she was called Snow White. The Queen was very proud of her own blond beauty and very envious of Snow White. Being something of a witch, she had a magic mirror. Each morning she would look into it and say, "Who is the most beautiful woman in the world?" The mirror would answer, "Snow White is the most beautiful woman in the world." This made the Queen so angry that she determined to be rid of the young girl.

She called a hunter to her and said, "Take Snow White out into the cold winter woods so far that she cannot find her way back." This the hunter did three times. Twice Snow White, weary and half-frozen, managed to retrace her steps and get home. The third time she was not so fortunate. She wandered through the icy forest paths until she was almost ready to drop with cold and fear. The wind swept through the pines, and frosty flakes fell like a mantle upon Snow White's shoulders. When she was about to give up and try no more, she saw a light ahead of her! What a joy to discover a tiny cottage!

She entered it. A bright fire was blazing on the hearth. The table was set with seven little bowls and seven stools. In the bedroom were seven little beds, each one as snug as a bird's nest. So weary was Snow White that she sank down upon one of them and went to sleep. Great was her surprise when she woke up to find standing about her bed seven strange little men with peaked caps and long beards. At first she was very much frightened. But they spoke so kindly to her that she was soon reassured.

They took her to the table. One of the little dwarfs, for dwarfs they were, sat on a log of wood and gave her his stool. Another ate from a large acorn and gave her his bowl. A third little dwarf, all rolled up in a soft moleskin, lay on the hearth, and gave her his bed.

The next morning Snow White told her story. All the seven dwarfs begged her not to go back to the wicked Queen, but to remain with them. That is just what she did. She cooked and baked and swept for the delighted little men while they were away at their various elfin tasks. At night when they came trooping home, they always brought her a present. There was never anything but joy and happiness in that funny little house, and the years passed with few misadventures. In the end a great prince found the little housekeeper. First he punished the wicked Queen and broke her magic mirror. Then he married Snow White, and they lived happy ever after. But she did not forget her companions, the gnomes, and the happy days they had spent together. And always they remained her faithful friends.

Thinking of this tale that he had heard in his childhood, Mr. Koralewsky used it on his lock. To the left you can see Snow White cooking for the little men. The table is all set, and the seven chairs drawn up to it. A tiny fellow, tugging at a carrot, is entering the house by an underground entrance near her. Another hop-o'-my-thumb is dragging in a hare twice as big as he is. What a fine stew it will make! Three little gnomes are on guard: one at the right side stands at a tiny post; one on the roof turns a diminutive knob; and the third at the very top, shameful to tell, has gone to sleep on duty, all under his toadstool umbrella. Because he has been so very careless, you can unlock the lock—if you know the secret and have turned the key. All you have to do is to give the toadstool a twist! For seven years Mr. Koralewsky was at work upon this story. You do not

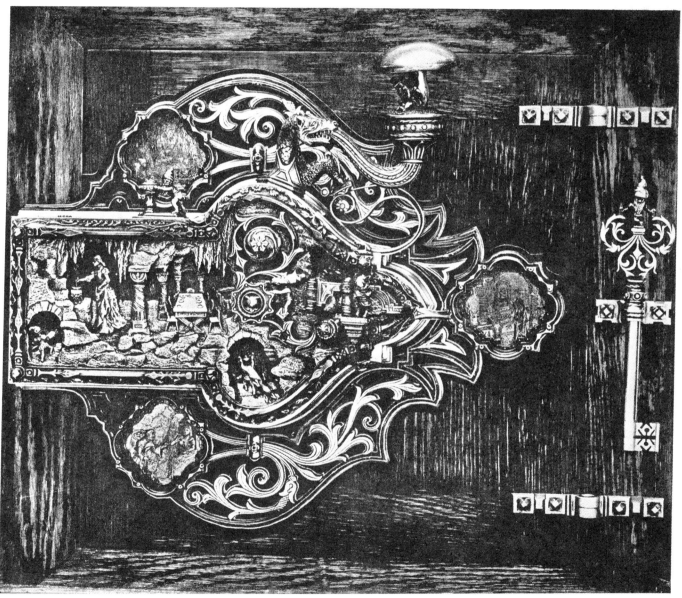

A Lock Telling the Story of Snow White, by Frank Koralewsky.

Courtesy of Mr. Koralewsky.

A Door Knocker, by Frank Koralewsky.

forge a fairy tale all in a minute. The many processes that have to be gone through in the forging are illustrated by a candelabra in three successive stages of finishing.

Looking as if they, too, might have stepped out of the story of "Snow White" are two little dwarfs standing guard on a pair of andirons. Both wear long hosen and rough little jerkins; both have pointed caps and long beards. The gnome who holds the poker is rather a serious fellow. Tending a fire is hard and grimy work

[204]

for him. The one who holds the bellows has a broad grin on his face; there is nothing he likes better than to scare up the sparks from their warm dens among the ashes and send them scurrying like red foxes up the sooty chimneypiece. It is well to note, too, the solid fire-dogs on which they stand, good heavy pieces of wrought iron, excellently adapted to their purpose.

Of all his delightful remembrances of gnomes none is more charming than the giant door knocker. If you want to use this knocker, you have to be brave enough to walk right up to it and pull the giant's whiskers. When you do so, the little gnome who is standing on his forehead gives him an awful blow on the nose with a tiny hammer. This sets the giant a-howling; the master of the house comes running; and the door is at once opened to you.

Most of the illustrations are of rather small objects; but were you to visit Mr. Koralewsky's plant, you would find great stairways, fountains, altar screens, grilles, and gates being made. Among the most beautiful of the latter is the gate now on the Crane estate in Ipswich, Massachusetts. It will show how the art of the ironworker can include the tiniest gnome or the largest bars and crosspieces of a great grille. Whether the object be massive or slight, there is no difference in the amount of care lavished upon it. Each thing is done as well as the workman's hand can do it. Each piece is stamped with the worth of the effort. Only so, says Mr. Koralewsky, can good work be done. Here in Boston to-day to the accompaniment of the hammer resounding on the anvil, the great world tradition is being carried on. Here you will find the honor of the craft of the ironworker in all its simplicity and power.

BIBLIOGRAPHY

The following list makes no attempt to furnish a comprehensive or even a well-balanced bibliography. It does, I think, cover those books consulted most frequently and may, perhaps, be of some use to those reading in similar fields.

Part I

Chapter I—*Weavers of Stories*

Champeaux, Alfred de—*Tapestry* (South Kensington Museum Handbook); Scribner, Welford, and Armstrong, 1878.

Hunter, George Leland—*Tapestries, Their Origin, History, and Renaissance*; John Lane Company, 1912.

Thomson, W. G.—*A History of Tapestry from the Earliest Times until the Present Day*; London, Hodder and Stoughton, 1906.

Candee, Helen Churchill—*The Tapestry Book*; Frederick A. Stokes Company, 1912.

Creasy, Sir Edward S., M.A.—*History of the Ottoman Turks*; Henry Holt and Company, 1878.

Demotte, G. J. (ed.)—*La Tapisserie Gothique*; Paris, Demotte, 1921-24.

Chapter II—*Brothers of the Quill*

Addison, Julia de Wolf—*Arts and Crafts in the Middle Ages*; The Page Company, 1908.

Bradley, John W.—*Illuminated Manuscripts* (2nd edition); London, Methuen & Company, Ltd., 1920.

Tymms, W. R.—*The Art of Illuminating as Practised in Europe from the Earliest Times*; London, Day and Son, 1860.

Herbert, J. A.—*Illuminated Manuscripts*; London, Methuen and Company, Ltd., 1911.

Millar, Eric G., F.S.A.—*English Illuminated Manuscripts of the XIVth and XVth Centuries*; Paris, G. van Oest, 1928.

Shaw, Henry, F.S.A.—*Dresses and Decorations of the Middle Ages*; 2 vols., London, Henry G. Bohn, 1858.

Chapter III—*Wood-Carvers of Long Ago*

Bond, Francis—*Wood Carvings in English Churches. I. Misericords*; London, Henry Frowde, Oxford University Press, 1910.

Howard, F. E. and Crossley, F. H.—*English Church Woodwork*; London, B. T. Batsford, 1917.

Cutts, Rev. Edward L., B.A.—*Scenes and Characters of the Middle Ages*; London, Alexander Moring, Ltd., The De La More Press, 1911.

Langeard, Paul—"Les plus belles stalles de France"; *Revue du Vrai et du Beau*, 25 November, 1925.

Lacroix, Paul—*Military and Religious Life in the Middle Ages and at the Period of the Renaissance*; D. Appleton and Company, 1874.

Milliken, William Mathewson—*A Gothic Abbot's Stall* in *The Bulletin of The Cleveland Museum of Art*, January, 1929.

Chapter IV—*The Armorer*

Dean, Bashford, Ph.D—*Helmets and Body Armor in Modern Warfare;* Yale University Press, 1920.

Dean, Bashford—*Notes on Arms and Armor*; Metropolitan Museum of Art, 1916.

Dean, Bashford—*Catalogue of a Loan Exhibition of Arms and Armor*; Metropolitan Museum of Art, 1911.

Dean, Bashford—*Catalogue of European Arms and Armor*; Metropolitan Museum of Art, 1905.

Ffoulkes, Charles, B.Litt, F.S.A.—*The Armourer and His Craft from the XIth to the XVIth Century;* London, Methuen and Company, Ltd., 1912.

Gilchrist, Helen Ives—*A Catalogue of the Collection of Arms and Armor Presented to The Cleveland Museum of Art by Mr. and Mrs. John Long Severance, 1924.*

Laking, Sir Guy Francis—*A Record of European Armour and Arms through Seven Centuries*; London, G. Bell and Sons, 1920. 5 vols.

Part II

Chapters V—IX

For the biographical material of this section, Vasari, mentioned as the "Old Historian," has been the chief source. I realize perfectly that he is more to be relied upon for entertainment than for scholarship. For this reason I have used the Blashfield-Hopkins edition, which is well edited and annotated. I hope that a reasonable degree of accuracy has been attained without losing the intrinsic quality of this delightful story-teller.

Blashfield, E. H. and E. W., and Hopkins, A. A. (ed.)—*Lives of Seventy of the Most Eminent Painters, Sculptors, and Architects*, by Giorgio Vasari, 4 vol.; Charles Scribner's Sons, 1913.

Symonds, John Addington (ed.)—*The Life of Benvenuto Cellini Written by Himself;* Brentano's, 1906.

Young, Colonel G. F.—*The Medici*; London, John Murray, 1909, 2 vols.

Brinton, Selwyn, M.A., F.R.S.A.—*The Golden Age of the Medici*; London, Methuen and Company, 1925.

Bode, Wilhelm—*Florentine Sculptors of the Renaissance*; Charles Scribner's Sons, 1928.

Powers, H. H., Ph.D.—*Mornings with Masters of Art*; Bureau of University Travel, 1912.

Brown, J. Wood, M.A.—*The Builders of Florence*; London, Methuen and Company, 1907.

SCOTT, LEADER—*Ghiberti and Donatello with Other Early Italian Sculptors*; Scribner and Welford, 1882.

JAMESON, MRS. ANNA—*Memoirs of the Early Italian Painters*; Houghton, Mifflin and Company, 1895.

SCOTT, LEADER—*Filippo di Ser Brunellesco;* London, George Bell & Sons, 1908.

CRUTTWELL, MAUD—*Donatello*; London, Methuen and Company, Ltd., 1911.

LELAND, CHARLES GODFREY—*Legends of Florence*; London, David Nutt, 1910.

MARQUAND, ALLAN—*Luca della Robbia*; London, Oxford University Press, 1914.

MARQUAND, ALLAN—*Andrea della Robbia;* London, Oxford University Press, 1922, 2 vols.

PART III

Chapter X—*Boston's Handyman*

GOSS, ELBRIDGE HENRY—*The Life of Colonel Paul Revere*; Howard W. Spurr, publisher, 1899, 2 vols.

BIGELOW, FRANCIS HILL—*Historic Silver of the Colonies and Its Makers*; The Macmillan Company, 1917.

EARLE, ALICE MORSE—*Home Life in Colonial Days*; The Macmillan Company, 1913.

An Outline of the Life and Works of Colonel Paul Revere; Towle Manufacturing Company, Newburyport, Mass., 1901.

MOSES, BELLE—*Paul Revere, the Torchbearer of the Revolution*; D. Appleton and Company, 1916.

DYER, WALTER A.—*Early American Craftsmen*; The Century Company, 1915.

Chapter XI—*A Wood-Carver of To-day*

MOSES, MONTROSE J. (*trans.*)—*The Passion Play of Oberammergau*; Duffield and Company, 1924.

BURTON, LADY ISABEL—*The Passion Play at Oberammergau*; London, Hutchinson and Company, 1900.

BERGENGREN, RALPH—*I. Kirchmayer, Wood-Carver*; in *The House Beautiful*, March, 1915.

Chapter XII—*Mastersmith*

GARDNER, J. STARKIE—*Ironwork*; London, Victoria and Albert Museum, Part I, 1927.

FFOULKES, CHARLES—*Decorative Ironwork from the XIth to XVIIIth Century*; London, Methuen and Company, Ltd., 1913.

HOEVER, OTTO—*An Encyclopædia of Ironwork*; London, Ernest Benn, Ltd., 1927.

BERGENGREN, RALPH—*An Adventure in the Medieval*; in *The House Beautiful*, January, 1915.